THE CIVIL WAR

Text
William J. Bradley

Photography
UPI/Bettmann
Culver Pictures Inc.
National Archives, Washington, D.C.

Design
Richard Richardson

Photographic Research
Leora Kahn
Kenneth Johnston

Commissioning Editor
Andrew Preston

Commissioning Assistant
Edward Doling

Editorial
Jane Adams

Production
Ruth Arthur
David Proffit
Sally Connolly

Director of Production
Gerald Hughes

Director of Publishing
David Gibbon

CLB 2398
© 1990 Colour Library Books Ltd, Godalming, Surrey, England.
All rights reserved.
This 1990 edition published by Military Press,
distributed by Outlet Book Company, Inc, a Random House Company,
225 Park Avenue South, New York, New York 10003.
Printed and bound in Italy.
ISBN 0 517 69325 9
8 7 6 5 4 3 2 1

THE CIVIL WAR

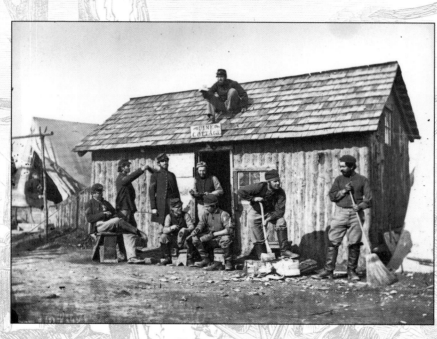

William J. Bradley

MILITARY PRESS

THE CIVIL WAR

THE CIVIL WAR

THE START OF THE WAR

The Nation and its New Wealth

The United States of America had been founded in 1776 as a balanced association of thirteen free and equal states. As time went by, however, new factors inevitably appeared, and they started to work against the maintenance of this delicate initial balance. In the first eighty-five years following the Declaration of Independence the frontiers were rolled very rapidly westwards, and twenty new and often virgin states were added to the USA by exploration, purchase or war – especially by the Mexican war of 1846-8. Meanwhile, the older-established states were making great leaps forward both technologically and financially. On different sides of the Mason-Dixon line this was to produce some very divergent political attitudes.

In the southern states the key new technology was the cotton gin, invented in 1793, which opened the way for the mass production of cotton on plantations worked by slave labor. Simultaneous advances in transportation and textile manufacturing opened an enormous European market for American cotton, which brought a new era of prosperity to the slave-owning states. The South's agricultural revolution therefore confirmed the traditional social hierarchy, but added a new scale to its wealth.

Southrons were increasingly liable to believe that their "peculiar institution" of chattel slavery was essential to this prosperity, although it was in some respects an institution whose sharper edges were now beginning to be softened. The spread of humanitarian principles brought some improvements in legal protection for slaves, and the growth of general wealth meant that they could often be given better working conditions. In places this even extended to increased wages, or freedom of movement, and very many slaves certainly had more skilled or interesting jobs than merely the drudgery of picking cotton. In any case, slaves almost everywhere formed a minority of the population; slave owners were a still smaller minority of the whites, plantation owners a minority of the slave owners. Most slave owners were smallholders with five slaves or less, operating at a very similar economic level to the majority of northern farmers. Nevertheless, general southern wealth and the militant southern self-image were built firmly on the institution of slavery, so there was absolutely no chance that it might somehow just fade away overnight if left to it own devices.

By contrast in the North, the technological developments accelerated an industrial and social revolution that created factories and bustling cities. Machines were changing the manufacture of most everyday commodities, and starting to introduce many new amenities. The capitalist ethic merged with traditional puritanism to encourage a booming free-trade market in which "progress" and mobility of labor were emphasized, and every laborer was worthy of his hire. Hence moral objections were increasingly raised against the backward-looking idea of slavery, until, by the 1830s, the abolitionist movement had become a respectable political force. A series of press and propaganda campaigns thereafter brought the issue into the very center of the national debate; not least when Harriet Beecher Stowe's *Uncle Tom's Cabin* became a best seller in 1852.

The moral fervor of the north was heightened by the influx of millions of European immigrants from the mid-1840s onwards. Many of these were Roman Catholics, which provoked heightened Protestant revivalism. They were also widely accused of alcohol abuse, which gave a great boost to the militant temperance movement. These apparently high-minded themes merged easily with a powerful American nationalist backlash against the immigrants, and created a form of sanctimonious exclusiveness that sought to define the national identity more closely than in the past. New immigrants from Europe could thus expect to win acceptance and full citizenship only by demonstrating their adherence to New England ideals, not least of which was belief in the sanctity of the USA, and by extension of the Union, itself.

Such attitudes extended into a condemnation of southerners for being allegedly violent, poorly educated, and dirty. Their slave-based society was seen as an "un-American" institution that stood as an affront to east coast values no less than to the Declaration of Independence. However, it was not merely the slave owners who were condemned in these terms since northern opposition to slavery was often combined with some deeply racist attitudes towards blacks. The slaves were often depicted as still more deeply "un-American" than their white masters, and some northern states even refused to admit any blacks at all, whether slaves or free men. Nor was resistance to slavery always high-minded, since it contained a strong strand of northern self-assertion against a South that was increasingly felt to exert too strong an influence in federal affairs, and an "alien" influence at that. As their population and industry continued to expand faster than those of Dixie, so the northern states came to believe that they deserved a greater voice in Congress. They wanted to revise the traditional equal balance of federal politics in order to protect their own manufacturing industries with tariffs, but without doing anything in return for the interests of southern agriculture. South Carolina had already threatened to secede over this issue in 1832-3, at which time this threat had carried weight. Businessmen had wanted a single market and peace every bit as much as they had wanted trade protection. A generation later, however, when secession seemed inevitable, the same businessmen would come out in favor of a single market rather than peace.

Naked power politics gave the North some clear reasons for wanting not only to reduce the southern voice in federal affairs, but also to dominate and control the course of development within the South itself. Although Massachusetts had itself contemplated secession during the war of 1812, by the 1860s the idea of the Union had evolved, implying a stronger degree of centralization than it had in the past. When the South replied that it would agree to go its own separate way, with neither side interfering in the affairs of the other, the North did not ultimately view this as an acceptable compromise. Naked power politics, once again, seemed to say that the USA would be much stronger if it remained united than if it were split, and such, in the event, has proved to be the case.

The Civil War was therefore a "War for the Union" quite as much, or more, than it was a war against slavery. It is scarcely surprising that the moral issue of slavery has often been seized upon as an emotive cause to conceal this underlying clash of interests, and to rally humanitarian support for the North. However, the fact that slavery *per se* was something less than the whole issue at stake is proved by the fact that its abolition was not even part of the original Union war aims, but crept in later. Many opponents of slavery would eventually fight for the South, just as many of its adherents would fight for the North.

Storms in Kansas and Harper's Ferry

In the years before the Civil War the Union included some industrialized northern states that were violently opposed to slavery, and some cotton-producing southern states that were violently in favor. However, there were also a series of new western territories applying for statehood, territories where plantation farming had not penetrated and where the economy still depended on more or less small-farm agiculture. Few of them had either the need or the desire to adopt slavery; yet many of them looked south down the Mississippi rather than east to New England for their cultural roots. The Old South also looked to them as a counterbalance against the expanding northeast. Although everyone agreed that their future was likely to be a bright one in the long term, its exact shape was still very much undefined. These frontier territories thus became the principal political battleground for the two opposing camps.

The first major clash had arisen around 1820 over Missouri and other territories similarly purchased from France during the Napoleonic era. In the end a compromise was agreed in Congress whereby Missouri became a slave state, but several other frontier areas did not. This reflected the general desire among politicians at that time to resolve the whole issue as amicably as possible, since it was so widely recognized as potentially explosive. A few years later the Democratic Party was to be founded in a similar spirit, drawing its members equally from both sides of the slavery debate.

By the end of the 1840s, however, the pressures caused by an escalating population, economic change and the Mexican war settlement were being felt to the full, culminating in the breakdown of the traditional party alignments over the slavery issue. Polarization had been evident in 1846, when the Wilmot Proviso attempted to ban slavery from new lands taken from Mexico. This measure had failed, but polarization continued. In 1850, in order to reduce it, Congressman Henry Clay of Kentucky proposed a new compromise for the ever-expanding frontier territories. He suggested that some of these territories should be allowed to adopt slavery if they wished to, and that the law should be reinforced to return fugitive slaves to their masters even if caught in non-slave states. However, California, pulsating with its recent gold rush, was to be free, and the trade in slaves was to be abolished in Washington DC. This compromise was accepted, as the Missouri compromise of 1820 had been, but this time there was a significantly sharper ground swell of resistance. William H. Seward of New York, especially, spoke out for a hardening anti-slavery position and evoked "a higher law" than the Constitution. When the Kansas-Nebraska Act of 1854 finally demolished the old party system, Seward emerged as a leading figure in a new "Republican" Party that was firmly sectarian and northern in its support. As such, its very existence made compromise with the South constitutionally more difficult than ever, thereby bringing war considerably nearer.

The Kansas-Nebraska Act itself was proposed by an ambitious Democratic senator from Illinois, Stephen A. Douglas. He hoped effectively to open those areas to slavery, even though they were north of the normal slave line, but without openly saying so. The formula used was to allow each territory to decide its own laws on the issue in the name of states' rights, local democracy, and squatter sovereignty. The Act was passed in the teeth of northern opposition that claimed these new territories were thereby being condemned to a backward economic structure that would close them to free enterprise and free labor. The opposition also drew emotional strength from the Fugitive Slave Law agreed in Clay's 1850 compromise, which had proved to be not only difficult to enforce but also an excellent amplifier for abolitionist propaganda.

On the ground in Kansas, immigrants were ranged on both sides of the debate, although supporters of slavery brought very few slaves with them, and the anti-slavery faction enacted legislation banning *any* black from even entering the state. There were soon armed clashes, blatant gerrymandering and rival state governments each claiming legitimacy. Sectarian guerrilla bands were established, some of them even equipped with artillery. This violence was reflected on the floor of the Senate in 1856 when a respresentative from South Carolina assaulted and injured a Senator from Massachusetts. Northerners were naturally fired up against the innate violence of the southern slave-owners, but the incident perhaps also helped blind them to both their own questionable tactics and to the very deep determination with which southern rights would be defended. In any event it failed to stop a two-year comic opera as each side in turn invented a new constitution for Kansas, only to have it thrown out either in Washington or by the now discredited processes of squatter democracy. To cut a very long story short, Kansas eventually entered the Union as a free state in 1861, but was immediately plunged into an intensified new round of its own long-standing civil war, especially along its southern border.

It is hard to see how the ideological confrontation of the 1850s could possibly have been defused unless either the South had abandoned slavery or the North had abandoned its hankering to dictate policy within every state and territory, southern as well as northern, not-yet-settled as well as long-occupied. There were deep constitutional issues at stake concerning how far the federal government's decisions were binding on state legislatures, and how far unrepresentative southern minorities could be allowed to determine federal decisions. This last issue was highlighted by the Dred Scott case of 1857 when the Supreme Court, where southern judges were in the majority, ruled against Scott, a slave who wanted his freedom because he had lived with his master for several years in non-slave areas. The Supreme Court's decision enraged northerners because it infringed the 1820 Missouri compromise demarcating slave and non-slave territories. It seemed to allow slavery to be practiced legally in anti-slavery states, and to symbolize the power of a minority of southerners to dictate policy against the mainstream of northern opinion.

The next major upsurge of emotion was sparked by a clear case of abolitionist aggression; the John Brown Raid of October 1859 against the Harper's Ferry armory. John Brown was a fanatical opponent of slavery who had won fame fighting as a guerrilla in Kansas. Now he wanted to bring the war closer to the southern states by setting up a base in Virginia to spark off a mass rising of slaves. For this he needed arms, so he and his band of eighteen men went to Harper's Ferry to steal them. The attack succeeded in capturing the armory, but it failed to win support among the slaves there, and the raiders were soon besieged by local militia and some federal marines commanded by a certain Colonel Robert E. Lee. After a fight in which seventeen people were killed, Brown was captured. He was duly tried, hung and hailed as a martyr by the abolitionist press. The fact that his assault was directed against a federal, rather than a specifically southern, installation was an irony conveniently forgotten by later singers of "The Battle Hymn of the Republic."

Lincoln, Secession, and War

The South was incensed by the John Brown episode, which seemed to show both the violence and the hypocrisy of the abolitionists. The Democratic Party split down the middle on sectional lines while many influential politicians, on both sides, increasingly insisted that secession was illegal. Hard-line Southerners replied that Massachusetts had thought

THE CIVIL WAR

it legal when it suited her in the past, and a sovereign state that had freely joined the Union might just as freely leave it. For them the question was now less a matter of "whether" secession would follow, but "when" it would. It only needed one more spark to ignite the powder keg.

That spark came when Abraham Lincoln was elected President a year later, in November 1860. Until then President James Buchanan, of Pennsylvania, had been seen as a compromise appointment acceptable to both sides of the Democratic Party. His opposition to secession was badly received in the South, but he had tempered it with a toleration of slavery where it already existed, and an indecisive refusal to contemplate coercion against any state that did secede. Lincoln, however, was known for his rather stronger views both against slavery and against disunion. He wanted a more active policy to reunite the "House Divided', and made it clear that, although he was not an outright abolitionist, he would like to push back the areas where slavery was permitted. He could not claim to speak for the South because he had won very few votes there, and had not even been a candidate in some parts. Worse still, in southern eyes, was the fact that he was a member of the sectional Republican Party, with many anti-slavery extremists standing behind him. Although he was seen as something of a moderate in the North, his election represented a very ominous weakening of the southern position within the federal government. Many Southerners felt that this would deal a death blow to their hopes of running their own affairs in future.

It could be argued that the essential interests of the southern states were by no means inevitably forfeit simply because Lincoln had been elected. Even if Kansas and the other frontier territories were forced to abandon slavery entirely, and if all slaves setting foot in the north were released from bondage immediately, that in itself did not automatically mean the destruction of the southern way of life. There was certainly a strong element of irrational fear and artificial excitement surrounding the election campaign, which agitators on both sides were quick to exploit. For example, they chose to hide the unspectacular but very significant fact that the Democrats, often southern sympathisers, still controlled Congress and the Supreme Court. If there had been no crisis, Lincoln might simply have become an entirely powerless president. Yet, for all that, it remains true that very few inhabitants of either the North or the South by this time really believed that things could continue as they were. Half-successful compromises could not cover up the very real differences between the two opposing outlooks forever. As with many marriages, it was because of the underlying unhappiness between the two sides, rather than for any more specific reason, that the final breakdown occurred. When they became tired of hurling insults, the partners exchanged blows instead, without at first fully realising the difference. Lincoln's election was thus merely a symbolic moment that happened to set the next stage of conflict in motion.

This next stage was Secession. The first to leave the Union, on December 20th 1860, was South Carolina, a state that had long taken the lead in suggesting this type of action. There was a brief pause to let the implications sink in, during which President Buchanan, then in his last few, fateful "lame duck" months in office, sent no clear deterrent signal that he would energetically repress the rebellion. South Carolina then demanded the surrender of all federal installations within her borders, notably the forts in Charleston Harbor. In response, it became known that both President Buchanan and the garrison commander, Major Robert Anderson, had decided to refuse the demand. The latter gathered all his men in Fort Sumter and, without wishing for bloodshed, continued to serve the US Government. However, when an unarmed ship was sent to resupply him on January 9th it had to retire after being fired on by the Southerners. These were arguably the first shots of the Civil War.

This sequence further heightened tension throughout the South,

where it was believed that a seceding state had every right to full sovereignty within its own territory. According to many, Anderson's action was itself tantamount to a declaration of war, although others believed his besiegers were to blame. However that may be, secession now became general throughout the Deep South. Between January 9th and February 1st 1861, South Carolina was joined by Mississippi, Florida, Alabama, Georgia, Louisiana and Texas. Their representatives met in Montgomery, Alabama, and agreed to form the Confederate States of America under the leadership of Jefferson Davis of Mississippi. Davis had great experience as an army officer and government minister, and in Confederate terms he was a political moderate. He was thus an excellent choice to be the southern President for the war that was now almost inevitably.

Matters hung in the balance for a few weeks as President-elect Lincoln worried out his policy up to and including his Inauguration Day on March 4th 1861. He hoped to win over those southern states that had not yet seceded, and also the moderates within those that had, by offering them the "carrot" that if they remained in the Union he would not take away their slaves. His "stick" was to repeat that secession was illegal under the Constitution, although, like Buchanan before him, he remained vague about what might be done to stop it. The overall effect of his statements was, therefore, ambiguous and failed to shock the Confederates into reconsidering, particularly since he also provocatively repeated that slavery was morally wrong and must not be allowed to spread. Lincoln cannot be accused of appeasement, but neither did he succeed in browbeating the opposition. He was perhaps little more clear-sighted than anyone else about the fast-moving and unprecedented events that were happening all around him.

He did at least feel obliged to make a new attempt to resupply Fort Sumter which, not unexpectedly, drew a southern ultimatum for the fort's surrender. When this was refused the Charleston batteries opened a bombardment of the fort at 4.30 am on April 12th, 1861. After thirty-four hours' firing the garrison capitulated – without having lost a man, but having participated in the start of a war.

Drawing the Battle Lines

The bombardment of Fort Sumter sparked a unanimous wave of northern indignation that took the South by surprise. Where they had expected a weak and divided reaction, they found a vengeful feeling that, in the words of Ulysses S. Grant, "There are but two parties now, traitors and patriots." Lincoln called for 75,000 militia and at last revealed that he was in fact ready to coerce the South with the full force of armed might.

This led to a new spate of secessions. Virginia, North Carolina, Tennessee and Arkansas left the Union between April 17th and May 20th, the first of these being a particularly rich prize for the South. Not only did Virginia furnish some of the Confederacy's most talented sons, but she also gave it a capital, Richmond, and a strategic avenue to the very gates of the enemy's capital in Washington DC. Virginia was to experience far more than its fair share of this war, and even suffered its own internal secession when West Virginia defected to the Union and eventually became a separate state. An attempt to regain it failed in July 1861, when the famous Union general George B. McClellan won small battles at Rich Mountain and Carrick's Ford.

In the immediate wake of the outbreak of war the Union government in Washington realised that it was itself in an exposed position, surrounded by the southern-sympathising state of Maryland. Troops were rushed forward from the north to defend it, but *en route* they had to pass through Baltimore, a center of secessionist agitation. On 19th April the mob turned out and stoned them, to which they replied with musketry. There was a crisis as Washington found itself cut off in hostile territory, although within a few days more men came down from Massachusetts and New York to secure the whole territory north of the Potomac for the Union, with Alexandria and Arlington soon being taken into the Washington defences. There were some other minor skirmishes across the Potomac, but by and large the two sides spent the next three months preparing their armies for the decisive battle in Virginia. As for Maryland, it accommodated itself to its northern masters, but sent enough men south to form several Confederate regiments. The last man to be killed in Lee's Army of Northern Virginia was a cavalryman from Maryland.

Meanwhile, the frontiers were being defined further west as other border states decided where their loyalties should rest. Kentucky remained neutral at first, being torn between love of both the south and of the Union. By September 1861, however, subtle Union diplomacy and impatient Confederate military advances into the state had combined to bring it out for the north. Many of her thereby "orphaned" citizens could nevertheless be found fighting for the Confederacy, and later in the war there was even to be a combat between two 4th Kentucky regiments, one from each side.

In Missouri sympathies were equally divided, but the firebrand Republican Nathaniel Lyon provoked a crisis by robbing the St Louis armory and firing on opposition demonstrators. He established a form of Union supremacy, and at the small battle of Boonville in June 1861 made the north of the state and the Mississippi river line secure. However, the interior was never completely tamed, even after the Union occupied the whole state early in 1862. A quarter of all the recruits furnished by Missouri during the war would fight for the South, while Lyon himself would be defeated and killed at the battle of Wilson's Creek in August 1861. This battle revealed the military incompetence of the overall Union commander of the West, the adventurer John C. Frémont, who was responsible for further disasters in the Shenandoah valley the following year, not to mention his involvement in scandals over arms contracts. He was at least the torchbearer for one devastatingly effective northern weapon which did much to win the West, if not the whole war, for Lincoln. At a time when the Confederates were still using an ineffective battering ram against the door of western politics, the Republicans found a key that opened it. By promising a land grant of 160 acres to every genuine settler in the new territories, they secured the loyalty of vast areas westwards from Ohio, not excluding the troubled state of Kansas which had been such a major catalyst of the war.

The importance of the West for Civil War strategy, however, lay less in the outcome of its pre-war politics than in its human and material resources. By securing the lion's share of these, the Union entered hostilities with a great advantage. It spent the next four years trying to increase this lead by pushing its borders ever further to the south while denying Confederate access to the same resources. Of particular significance would be the campaign to seize the Mississippi along its entire length, thereby splitting the Confederacy in two, driving its traffic from the great waterway itself, and preventing the inflow of men, cattle and imported goods from Arkansas and Texas.

A similar process was envisioned for the 3,500 miles of Confederate coastline further to the east. In his so-called "Anaconda Plan," made soon after the start of the war, the veteran general Winfield Scott outlined a total blockade of the South. This plan effectively cut it off from the outside world and deprived it of all the many raw materials and manufactured goods that it would need. The Union enjoyed the great advantage that most of the prewar navy had remained loyal. It was to be an invaluable asset, not only for moving and supplying armies in the field, but for seizing bases on southern coasts from which the blockade could be maintained. Fort Sumter itself would have been very useful for

this, if it could have been held. Fort Pickens in Pensacola, Florida, still remained an unsubdued Union stronghold, and would continue as such throughout the whole war, as would Fort Monroe on the Yorktown Peninsula in Virginia. Nevertheless, more bases, and many more ships were needed. Therefore, a series of coastal campaigns were planned, and, despite setbacks, were gradually put into effect. Scott's Anaconda plan took some years to come into full operation, but it was eventually fully to develop the level of encircling, crushing power that its designer had wanted.

Others in the Union camp found Scott's plan too cautious, defensive and slow. It lacked the immediate retribution of a decisive battle in the field, and scarcely allowed for the surprises that time might bring, such as the entry of Great Britain into the war on the side of her cotton-growers. The northern press was, therefore, impatient, and wanted the army to march "Forward to Richmond" at once. By advancing into Virginia the northern hosts could simultaneously protect their exposed Washington bastion, free the downtrodden slaves, and extirpate the traitor in his lair. This analysis was excellent in political theory and in its patriotic aspirations, but unfortunately deficient in simple military practicalities, as we shall see.

Opinions on Confederate strategy were no less divided than those in the Union, with some, such as General Pierre T. Beauregard, urging the offensive, and others, such as President Davis or General Joseph E. Johnston, urging defense. Many argued that the South's aim was merely to survive intact and win international recognition as a sovereign state; after a while the North would surely give up and make peace. There was therefore no need to invade the North, and possibly be seen as unnecessarily aggressive – particularly in view of the northern superiority of over two to one in mobilizable manpower, and far greater than that in industrial production. Others, however, argued that it was precisely because of this northern superiority that an offensive was vital. It was only by carrying the war to the Northerners, and making them pay a price, that they might be persuaded to give up the fight. Besides, an invasion might secure valuable supplies for the South or damage northern industries. The Confederacy certainly had no guarantee that a passive defensive posture would be enough to make the North desist; furthermore the European powers might interpret it as a sign of weakness.

The Armies Assemble

As the strategists gathered their thoughts and the trumpets sounded for the start of the fighting, the two armies looked into their enlistment rolls and inventories to find just what assets they could call upon, and what they still lacked. The picture was not a bright one, since the regular peacetime US army had included little more than 16,000 trained men, almost all of whom stayed with the North, and a maximum of 3,000 officers, of whom almost a third went over to the Confederacy. This did not constitute an adequate enough force for even one small campaign, let alone a full continental war with many fronts, and it left most parts of the service chronically short of expertise. The Confederates, for example, had just thirteen trained engineer officers at the start of the war from whom to draw supervisors for all their coastal and land-based fortifications, as well as other technicalities such as military signalling and topography. They were fortunate that one of these was Robert E. Lee of Virginia, a master craftsman in warfare and one of the world's all-time great commanders, but his excellence shone out all the more clearly because he had so few rivals.

In the face of this manpower crisis both sides resorted to the mass levy of a volunteer militia, citizen soldiers who at first were contracted to serve for only a few months or a year. Not only did they bring no military experience with them when they enlisted, and had to learn everything from scratch, but, unless they could be persuaded to re-enlist, they would take their training back home with them again after a very short time. Even eighteen months into the war this still caused a great deal of manpower turbulence, although by then most volunteers were signing on for three years' duty, and in April 1862 the Confederates had already introduced conscription. As for the officers, most were pure civilians: local landowners, businessmen or politicians who had helped raise units, or had been elected by their peers. Without anything like enough properly trained officers or men, therefore, the regiments took a long time to settle down and learn how to fight.

It also took time for regimental organizations to become standardized, since at the start of the war there were many local improvizations and "personal" units raised by individuals, such as the multifarious "Zouave", "Garibaldi" or "Highland" outfits in New York. In the South, especially, privately assembled companies of up to a hundred men were common, each with its own distinctive name. A number of these might later be grouped together as a regiment or sometimes even as a non-regulation all-arms "legion" – but in the face of such diversity it took a long time for a centralized military system to emerge.

When it came to armaments, there were enough to equip the first flood of recruits – maybe half a million firearms in the South and twice that in the North. However, the vast majority of these were obsolescent smoothbore muskets. The Union could find little more than 100,000 modern rifled muskets, and the Confederacy just 35,000. The scale and pace of the mobilization were also such that these arms had soon all been distributed, and a variety of expedients had to be used to find more. A selection of old and new guns were bought in Europe; recruits were encouraged to bring their own hunting weapons or duelling pistols; and pikes, machetes or cutlasses sometimes had to be issued in lieu of any gun at all. While the directors of government arsenals scratched their heads to find ways of increasing the normal total continental production rate of about 15,000 weapons per year, free enterprise industrialists sniffed a profit and started to advertise both their defective old stock and untested new inventions.

As regards artillery the problem was still more acute and the South, in particular, soon found itself in a deep manufacturing crisis. Not only did it never have quite enough cannon or ammunition for its field armies, especially of the more modern rifled types, but it lacked the heavy industry needed to build a navy or to sustain existing railroads at full efficiency. In the North the industrial mobilization went ahead far more successfully, and their armies, if anything, suffered the embarrassment of having too much equipment. At the battle of the Wilderness in 1864 General Grant could allow himself the luxury of sending home 122 of his cannons, because they excessively obstructed the roads.

With all these difficulties to overcome, it is remarkable that the two sides could nevertheless field a total of over 100,000 men between them in the Eastern theater for the First Manassas, (or First Bull Run) campaign, only three months after the bombardment of Fort Sumter. The aim of the Union forces, under General Irvin McDowell, was to march "Forward to Richmond" and stamp out the Confederacy by capturing its capital. The Confederates, under Generals Johnston and Beauregard, wanted to turn the invaders out of Virginia, and if possible go on to capture Washington itself.

The campaign was an offensive by superior Union forces, but they failed to concentrate properly on the battlefield. The Confederates' staffwork and operational mobility were better, although on the day of the battle, July 21st 1861, McDowell did manage to execute a neat turning movement around their left flank. For a moment it looked as though he had won a quick and economical victory, but he soon found that faulty staffwork continued to dog his footsteps. McDowell's attack lost co-ordination while the Confederates, using wigwag semaphore to summon reinforcements to the threatened point, consolidated their defence. It was at this point that General Thomas J. Jackson won his famous nickname of "Stonewall" for the stalwart barrier he placed in front of the Yankee advance, although some detractors have suggested that it originated more from a complaint that he was simply standing motionless and stonewalling requests to advance into the fray.

At least the northern assault did fall apart and eventually, after a brutal firefight, started to give way. The retreat turned into a rout as the Union army swept aside Washington tourists, who had come to watch the fun, and streamed away to the rear. This was the best possible outcome for the vulnerable young Confederacy, since it reassured them that their army was competent and persuaded doubters to back the war more wholeheartedly. Unfortunately, however, General Beauregard failed to thrust forward into the decisive pursuit that might have given him Washington. Union doubters also rallied, and Congress approved the raising of a million new troops. Never again was the Union capital to lie so defenceless before a Southern army, although this was of course not clear at the time.

The First Two Years of Campaigning

From the Peninsula to Chancellorsville
Campaigns in Virginia

First Manassas persuaded the North that the professional soldiers were right to lay stress on careful drilling, acclimatization and long training before the army entered the field. This was all the more important because the three month men who had enlisted at the start of the war now had to go home. A serious winter of army building therefore lay ahead for the new Union commander, McClellan. As the Napoleon of the minuscule West Virginia campaign, and a scientific commentator on European warfare before 1861, McClellan had many of the organizational and analytical skills that were required. He built up the Army of the Potomac into a large and technically formidable fighting machine. However, he did have some important blind spots.

In organizational terms, he neglected the cavalry and the staff. He relied for his intelligence mainly on the Pinkerton detective agency, which had good information on Confederate numbers but which, in order not to short-change the client, added half as many again, in case there might be some unknown units. The result was that McClellan consistently overestimated enemy numbers and became even more cautious than he would otherwise have been, which was already quite cautious enough. He was one of a whole generation of West Point graduates trained to believe in the value of fortification in battle, and the need to avoid frontal attacks. It also soon became clear that in moments of crisis he was personally liable to lose his decisively "Napoleonic" grip on events.

All this emerged in March 1862, when the Army of the Potomac launched its second, long-awaited offensive against the Confederate capital. McClellan decided to approach by sea, along the Yorktown Peninsula to the east of Richmond, rather than cross-country along the direct route from Washington. This had the advantage of bypassing the difficult march through Virginia, and past Manassas of shameful memory; but it also split his forces into three disconnected parts. McClellan could not take the whole army with him because a large garrison had to be left behind to cover Washington. In addition, a secondary campaign was planned in the Shenandoah valley to secure the western flank of the operation. By choosing the amphibious option, therefore, McClellan successfully reduced his initially crushing numerical superiority down to a level the Confederates could handle.

As he gingerly approached Richmond along bad roads through wooded terrain, McClellan was careful to dig in at every opportunity. Even then he was attacked by General Johnston's outnumbered forces on May 31st 1862 at Seven Pines, (or Fair Oaks). McClellan suffered a psychological jolt but eventually beat off the enemy, inflicting 6,000 casualties and wounding Johnston himself. McClellan thereafter remained inactive, being thrown ever deeper into indecision by the first of J. E. B. Stuart's epic cavalry raids on the rear guard of his army. Then, towards the end of June, the Confederates, still outnumbered but with morale high, and now commanded by "Massa Bob" Lee, returned to the offensive in a series of assaults known as the Seven Days' Battle.

Military experts have shaken their heads at Lee's rashness in making these attacks against superior numbers of well-entrenched Union soldiers, and have talked of the hotheadedness and unthinking "warrior ethos" of the slave-owning southern culture. Lee's staffwork fell to pieces repeatedly during the week's fighting, and he suffered some 20,000 casualties, a quarter of his army, while inflicting just 16,000 on the enemy. Only once, at Gaines's Mill on June 27th 1862, did he fully carry a Union trench line; in the other attacks he was beaten off. On the face of it he does not seem to have shown very good generalship. What the experts miss, however, is the fact that he won the battle as a whole, and by his unrelenting pressure left his opponent in a state of demoralization. After each successful defense McClellan instinctively pulled back, until he came to see his devastating final defense of Malvern Hill on July 1st as merely a covering action for an evacuation and return to Washington. Richmond had been delivered, by blood but also by bluff, from the most dangerous move that would be mounted against it before its final fall in 1865.

Part of the Union problem in the spring of 1862 lay in the mind of its commander, but another part lay in the divided command arrangements between the army in the Peninsula and the government in Washington. Lincoln did not fully trust McClellan, and was concerned at the threat to the flank of his capital from the Shenandoah valley. It was here that Stonewall Jackson had conducted his classic "Valley Campaign" between late March and early June, establishing his reputation as a genius of maneuver and surprise. He moved rapidly and secretly between northern formations that were out of touch with each other and under different commands, defeating each in turn. Such prowess in marching did Jackson's infantry possess, in fact, that it became known as "foot cavalry," establishing a standard of toughness and endurance that has seldom been matched. With rarely more than 15,000 of these excellent

troops, he was able to distract the north's attention, and almost 60,000 of its men, away from the Peninsular Campaign. Not only that, but he even managed to slip away from the valley with his own men in time to join Lee for the Seven Days' Battle. It all added up to a virtuoso demonstration of the principle of economy of force.

Once Lee and Jackson had seen off McClellan from the gates of Richmond, their troops enjoyed the great boost to morale that comes from victory. Despite its ever inadequate supply service and over-personal staffwork, the Confederate army was shaking out into full maturity as a flexible and battle-hardened fighting force. Against it the Union put up a succession of inexperienced armies that did not improve when they tasted defeat. The latest of these was now moving south into Virginia, under the command of the braggart General John Pope, who had fought successfully in the western theater but who now seemed out of his depth in the "big league" of the East. He tried to demonstrate an energetic approach by announcing his headquarters would always be "in the saddle," but found that the dry wits in his new command were unimpressed, since they had understood this was where one normally kept one's hindquarters ...

By mean of an echeloned march led by Jackson, Lee's army bundled Pope from Cedar Mountain, on the Rapidan, back towards his supply base at Manassas. Accelerating the pace to forestall the arrival of Union reinforcements, Jackson swung round behind him and reached the supplies first, and then started a Second Battle of Manassas, Second Bull Run, from dawn on August 29th 1862. At first, as he stood along a railroad embankment under a series of Union attacks, Jackson was heavily outnumbered However, the next day General James S. Longstreet arrived with the remainder of Lee's army to relieve him, and together they chased Pope back in disarray towards Washington. Out of the 63,000 Union troops in the battle there were 14,000 were made casualty, as against 10,000 out of 54,000 Confederates. The Lee-Jackson-Longstreet combination had found its optimum rhythm, combining speed and boldness with a shrewd assessment both of the situation and of the enemy's psychology.

After Second Manassas the Confederates tried to exploit the initiative they had won by invading Maryland to threaten Washington from the north. They did not get far, however, since McClellan was on hand with his army from the Peninsula and, by chance, he had intercepted a copy of Lee's orders. Acting with uncharacteristic decisiveness, he threw his forces into the pursuit and brought the Confederates to bay at Antietam Creek, Sharpsburg on September 17th. There they fought the battle known as "America's bloodiest day," in which some 13,700 southern and 12,350 northern soldiers were made casualties within the space of about twelve hours. The fighting was between closely-packed ranks and at short range, with few of the troops bothering to dig in for protection.

On this occasion Lee was fighting on the defensive, with the Potomac to his rear and not all his army concentrated. He should have been destroyed. Initially he had fewer than 20,000 men pitted against over 70,000, with reinforcements just before the battle and throughout the day eventually giving him around 40,000. Lee need not have worried, however, since McClellan's attacks were poorly co-ordinated, and his renewed caution and uncertainty led him to hold back a third of his force in reserve. This allowed the Confederates to meet him on terms of near parity in the front line, and, although they reeled under the weight of his assaults, they were eventually able to hold their own. Once again, therefore, McClellan "snatched defeat from the jaws of victory." Nor did he redeem the situation, as he might easily have done, by mounting an energetic pursuit when Lee started to withdraw. He sat and did nothing until a frustrated government finally had him replaced by the ingenious and bewhiskered General Ambrose E. Burnside.

THE CIVIL WAR

Burnside followed Lee back to the Rapidan-Rappahannock river line, from which Pope had been chased in August, but without being able to capitalise on Confederate weakness or dispersion. He soon found himself facing a strongly defended linear position at Fredericksburg, from which Lee could move rapidly to counter flank moves. It was despite his doubts, therefore, that Burnside resolved to make a direct frontal assault at Fredericksburg, with the main action starting on 13th December 1862.

The result was another blood bath, with almost as many Union casualties as at Antietam, but only half as many Confederate. The fighting was especially concentrated at the foot of Marye's Hill. Here some 30,000 men attacked on a front just 1,000 yards wide, over open ground, against a well protected position ranged in several tiers up the hillside. Confederate fire halted the front line at a range of around a hundred yards, then there was chaos as succeeding lines became hopelessly entangled with each other. Most of the attackers went to ground without having a chance to organize themselves or to renew the forward momentum, and when new formations were added they merely made matters worse.

There was a similar story further downstream, where Jackson held off the attack by an active defense, and there the battle rested for thirty-six hours until Burnside retired quietly under cover of darkness. A month later he tried to outflank the Fredericksburg defences from the West; this time he became bogged down in terrible weather before he even made contact with the enemy. This "mud march" discredited him as commander of the Army of the Potomac, although he continued to command a corps for most of the rest of the war.

Command of the Army of the Potomac was handed to Joseph E. Hooker, whose name has, perhaps unfairly, entered the language due to the interest shown by his Division towards a certain class of lady in Washington. At the start of 1863, however, he gave the army a much-needed administrative shake-up, and even took steps towards improving the cavalry and staff that McClellan had neglected. Then, when better weather arrived, he repeated the flanking maneuver Burnside had attempted in the "mud march," Hooker ensuring that this time it advanced a bit further than before.

Hooker successfully marched some 73,000 men around Lee's left, across the Rappahannock and into the woodland that is encouragingly known as "the Wilderness." He established his HQ at Chancellorsville and hoped to surprise the Confederates by attacking their rear with the main body of his army, whilst Sedgwick's 40,000 men launched a diversionary frontal attack from the direction of Fredericksburg. All this could well have added up to a spectacular victory, if only Hooker had had the courage of his convictions. Instead, however, he issued conflicting sets of counter-orders that wasted most of May 1st 1863, thus handing the initiative back to an enemy who was only too ready to seize it. Lee was already hastening forward from the Fredericksburg position with most of his army, determined to attack. On arrival in the Wilderness he found the Union forces well entrenched, but Jackson suggested detaching a heavy force to outflank them from the west. Lee agreed and, in one of the boldest decisions of military history, split his already inferior force into two. As he had against McClellan in the Peninsula, Lee gambled that by putting a brave face on things and attacking, he might appear to be much stronger and more confident than he really was.

The ruse worked; when Jackson unleashed his assault towards dusk the next day, he spread surprise and consternation throughout the Union ranks. Sigel's Germans streamed to the rear and, in the days before "teutonic" had become synonymous with "military efficiency," were made a laughing stock. It was no laughing matter for northern hopes, however, since the whole incident undermined Hooker's resolution. He "lost faith in Hooker" and ordered a retreat, even though he still held a potentially winning hand. By accident Jackson himself had been mortally wounded by one of his own sentries in the very hour of triumph. Sedgwick was in the process of pushing through the Fredericksburg lines that had held out for so long in the past. Hooker himself still enjoyed a large superiority in numbers. However, it was all to no avail, for Hooker stayed on the defensive while Lee made another rapid movement to contain Sedgwick, leaving just 25,000 troops to contain Hooker's 75,000. This clinched the battle for the Confederates who, with around 13,000 casualties, suffered *less* for their boldness than did the northern army with 17,000 casualties. In the aftermath of this result Hooker was replaced as commander by General George G. Meade, who was a less imaginative and colourful man than any of his predecessors, but was thus perhaps less prone to their violent changes of mood.

The Chancellorsville campaign also marked the end of the first intensive year of fighting in the eastern theater. The sheer number of operations in such rapid succession, combined with the speed of the movements, is surely as breathtaking for the student of warfare as it must have been exhausting for the participants. Over this year Lee's Confederates had unmistakably asserted their military prowess, disposing of no less than four Union commanders in turn – Pope, McClellan, Burnside and Hooker. They had saved Richmond and kept Washington nervous but, ultimately, they never succeeded in breaking the deadlock. Despite everything, Lee had never enjoyed the type of superiority in men and *equipment* that he needed for a decisive victory. By mid-May 1863 his brilliant maneuvers had failed to move the general battle line forward from where it had been in May 1862, or even from where it had been a year before that. It was a frustrating and unfair reward for so much sacrifice and effort, one that must have helped goad him forward into his next campaign, the offensive thrust into Pennsylvania that would bring him to Gettysburg.

Closing the Coastline

The "Anaconda Plan" called for a blockade of Confederate coasts to prevent both the export of currency-earning cotton and the import of vital war materials. At first this blockade had a negligible effect, and even by the end of the war perhaps half the blockade runners were still able to get through. One estimate suggests that only fourteen per cent of all blockade runners were intercepted over the war as a whole. Nevertheless, ordinary traders, especially if they had large and slow ships, were deterred from taking the risk. The blockade did therefore have a powerful effect in restricting the Confederate economy, especially since the Union often captured ports as well as stopping ships from using them. This meant that goods were landed at ever fewer places, which intensified the pressure on the South's never efficient internal distribution system to the point where it broke down completely.

As time went on, furthermore, some other important effects of the blockade were noticed, including the South's embarrassing dependence upon European shipyards for blockade runners and commerce raiders. This source of supply could of course eventually be cut off by northern diplomatic pressures on London or Paris, thereby complicating Confederate dealings with those governments. There was also a major threat of amphibious landings on southern shores, which meant that a relatively small Union deployment of forces in coastal garrisons led to a relatively large allocation of Confederate troops to contain them. It has been estimated that by the start of 1863 Jefferson Davis was maintaining some thirty-two per cent of his army in these duties, while Lincoln had similarly committed only twenty per cent of his army.

Many small coastal operations were mounted. At first a major effort was made in North Carolina, with the seizure of Hatteras Inlet in August

1861, Roanoke Island in February 1862, then New Bern. These beachheads were expanded inland and linked together later in the year. They were positioned so as to threaten Richmond from the rear, and attracted considerable countermoves from the defense. Less spectacular, perhaps, but no less logical for the Anaconda Plan, were the captures of Port Royal, Beaufort and Fort Pulaski between Savannah and Charleston; Fernandina, St Augustine, and PENSACOLA itself in Florida. Ship Island, Mississippi, strategically located between the key ports of Mobile and New Orleans also suffered the same fate. Leaving Wilmington, NC, as the only major Confederate dock left unmarked.

Norfolk, Virginia had always been watched from Fort Monroe, but in the spring of 1862 it became the scene of intensified action. Before McClellan brought his army forward to the Peninsula, the Union navy was at first caught out by the activities of the novel Confederate ironclad, *Merrimac*. Bursting out of harbor on March 8th, she sank some of the blockading squadron before retiring for the night. Next day, however, she found that the Union had brought up an ironclad of its own, the experimental *Monitor*. The two vessels fought it out for three hours, but neither was able to damage the other. Armor had improved faster than armor-piercing shell, and the result was a standoff behind which the northern blockade could be re-imposed.

As the first clash of ironclads, the epic duel between *Merrimac* and *Monitor* stands as a milestone in naval history. They were by no means the most advanced ships of their day, since much larger ironclads had already been purpose-built in Europe. However, they were ready on hand at the scene of the fighting, and they pointed the way to a revolution in American warship design. The Confederacy soon had to drop out of this race, especially when Norfolk was evacuated on May 9th and *Merrimac* was destroyed two days later, but the Union pressed ahead and built many bigger and better versions of *Monitor*. They were used for riverine warfare, notably at Vicksburg, and also in operations at sea. An excessive faith in their powers, however, sometimes led the US Navy to waste them in fruitless bombardments of coastal fortifications that proved no more vulnerable than had *Merrimac* herself.

After the ironclad duel in Hampton Roads, perhaps the most important maritime event of 1862 was Admiral David G. Farragut's opening of the Mississippi at New Orleans. He successfully ran the gauntlet of the forts at the mouth of the river, seized the city and then landed General Benjamin F. Butler's army. It was the richest prize the North had won so far, and the strategic implications were enormous. New Orleans represented an important foothold for Yankee propaganda in the very heart of the Deep South, and, equally, a major outlet for cotton and other trade. Without the town the Confederacy could no longer use the Mississippi, and was in danger of being split in two along that river line. The danger was quickly underlined when Farragut twice promenaded his fleet as far upstream as Vicksburg, which was destined to become the primary bastion of southern hopes in the West. Union ground forces also took Baton Rouge, but their progress up the Mississippi was soon blocked by the resistance of Port Hudson. It was to hold out until a few days after Vicksburg itself fell to General Ulysses S. Grant's attack from upriver in July 1863.

More locally to New Orleans a number of other land campaigns were mounted by the Union towards the Opelousas and even the Red River. These had little more success than did the short-lived seizure of Galveston, Texas, towards the end of 1862, though the campaigns were renewed with better results during the following year.

Closing the Western River Lines

If the South was badly wrong-footed by Union supremacy at sea, it also sustained huge early damage through Union domination of the river systems in the western theater. These were of especially great importance as highways of communication, since the population was less densely distributed than in the East, with a correspondingly less well-developed infrastructure of road and rail transportation. The side which controlled the rivers could therefore move far more freely than the side which was restricted to overland operations alone. This, taken together with the North's technological and material superiority in railroads, gave it a vital edge in strategic mobility, despite the more compact central position enjoyed by the Confederacy.

Following his initial forays in Missouri, Frémont had been replaced as Union commander in the West by General Henry W. Halleck, a prewar writer of military textbooks, known as "Old Brains" for his owlish intellectualism. Although personally less than inspiring, Halleck nevertheless possessed a very clear understanding of the strategic problems, and quickly set a most devastating campaign in motion. He saw that he held the initiative having a total of some 90,000 men in secure bases at St Louis and Louisville, and a concentrated striking force, under Grant, holding the key junction between the Mississippi, Ohio, Tennessee and Cumberland Rivers. Against this the Confederates, commanded by General Albert Sidney Johnston, only had around 43,000 troops. These were badly overstretched in a 400-mile cordon defense that required them to man a scattered chain of outposts stretching up the Mississippi from Memphis to Columbus, then up the Cumberland and Tennessee Rivers with a bastion in Bowling Green, Kentucky, and a link with West Virginia at Cumberland Gap.

The opening move was made by Grant against Fort Henry, the badly-fortified key to the Tennessee River. Enjoying excellent co-operation from Commodore Andrew H. Foote's riverine flotilla, Grant captured the fort quickly on February 6th 1862. Then, not without administrative difficulties, he marched overland to Fort Donelson on the Cumberland River, where a far more serious siege had to be undertaken. By 16th February Grant was nonetheless in a position to make his famous demand for "no terms except unconditional and immediate surrender," from which it was widely surmised that the "US" in his initials stood for "Unconditional Surrender."

The fall of Forts Henry and Donelson was a body blow to the Confederacy, denying it access to Kentucky and giving freedom of the waterways to the Union. Soon afterwards General Don Carlos Buell consolidated northern control of the Cumberland River by seizing Nashville, while Pope advanced down the Mississippi to capture Columbus and "Island Number Ten" at New Madrid. Within two months, therefore, Lincoln's western armies had secured an advance of at least fifty miles on all fronts.

Wishing to exploit these victories, Halleck had already ordered Grant forward to Pittsburg Landing, the nearest point on the Tennessee River from which the railroad junction at Corinth could be attacked. If Corinth were taken, Confederate rail communications between Memphis and Chattanooga would be cut, and east-west movements diverted along the much longer, rambling and incomplete lines through central Alabama or even via Mobile on the coast. The Confederates were fully sensitive to the danger, however, and were hastily concentrating a still stronger army at Corinth itself. With this force they advanced on Grant's unfortified camp around Shiloh church, taking it by surprise on April 6th 1862 with superior numbers, in what was perhaps the south's most auspicious opening to any battle of the war.

Like many of the other battles in the war, however, the battle of Shiloh soon degenerated into an uncoordinated and bloody mess. The Union line was surprised and badly battered, but it did not break. The difficulty of holding together the southern assault was compounded by the encumbered woodland terrain, by the inexperience of the young soldiers, and by the fatal mischance that carried off their leader, Albert Sidney Johnston, at the crucial moment. By dusk the Confederates had advanced three miles into Grant's position, but had failed to throw him into the river. Grant was then to receive massive reinforcements during the night, with the arrival of some of Buell's forces from Nashville. The initiative slipped away from the Confederates, and they retreated during the second afternoon, leaving some 10,700 casualties compared with 13,700 for the Union. These losses were on a scale that was fully comparable to those at Antietam, and they were even more devastating if the smaller size and lesser experience of the western armies is taken into account. Neither side could afford many more Shilohs, and both were to be more circumspect and cautious thereafter.

After Shiloh Halleck himself arrived to lead a painfully prudent advance on a Corinth that was equally prudently evacuated by Beauregard, although the latter thereby incurred the displeasure of Jefferson Davis, and consequently resigned. General Braxton S. Bragg assumed his mantle and began a policy of mounting raids against northern supply lines. This was quickly to become the classic type of western operation, causing untold delays and frustrations to the Union during the middle period of the war, but rebounding against the South towards the end with Sherman's march through Georgia and Wilson's through Alabama. It was a style of warfare particularly suited to the Western theater, where transportation was so difficult, since by rapid movements a raiding force could break away from the restrictions of formal logistics. Because it would not have to stand and occupy territory, it could to a large extent live off the land, and wreak havoc with the formal logistics of the enemy. Small bands of cavalry under intrepid leaders, such as Nathan B. Forrest or John H. Morgan, were able to make unassailable forays against Union railroads and supply dumps far behind the battle lines. These went a long way towards ensuring that the spectacular northern advances of the spring of 1862 could not be properly resumed until almost two years had passed.

In the late summer of 1862 Bragg mounted the first raid on a larger scale, using infantry and artillery as well as cavalry. Starting at Chattanooga he bypassed the Union forces in Tennessee to the east, and lunged for their supply bases in the heart of Kentucky. This movement was also intended to join up with General E. Kirby Smith's advance on Lexington from Knoxville. At first the operation went well, and by the time Bragg and Smith had almost reached the gates of Louisville they had caused Buell to retire from the Tennessee River line with most of his troops. The two Confederate forces failed to concentrate, however, and at Perryville on October 8th Bragg found himself with around 20,000 men, very short of supplies, facing twice as many enemy troops. After a scrappy fight he withdrew far, and fast. He fled south through Knoxville and Chattanooga and then north again to Murfreesboro on Stone's River. There he awaited the cumbersome advance of Buell's army, now commanded by General William S. Rosecrans who had just won kudos by his defense in the second battle of Corinth, on October 3rd – 4th.

The battle of Murfreesboro represented the high-water mark of another "raid" into northern territory, similar to the Perryville operation in its conception but rather less ambitious in execution. Bragg enjoyed many of the advantages of fighting on his own chosen ground, and his cavalry effectively blinded an enemy who did not on this occasion greatly outnumber the Confederates. On December 31st, therefore, Bragg scorned to dig fieldworks and started the battle by launching a powerful assault on the Union right flank. As at Shiloh, the Confederate offensive won intial success and pushed the enemy back two miles, but then started to fall apart before they could be annihilated. Overnight the defense was consolidated, and beat off all subsequent attacks until Bragg withdrew at the end of January 3rd, 1863. He found himself reenacting in Tennessee a similar scenario to Burnside's tactical failure at Fredericksburg two weeks earlier, although in this case the balance of casualties was marginally in favor of the attack. Bragg had suffered some 11,000 casualties compared with almost 13,000 inflicted on the enemy.

Murfreesboro marked "the end of the beginning" in the West, after which the center of attention would move to the siege of Vicksburg. The Confederacy would never again seize the initiative quite so firmly as had Bragg in his two raids north, although it would continue to make many more raids, both great and small, right up to the end of the war. Unfortunately for southern hopes, however, the North would now begin to reply with some counterraiding of its own.

The Political Background in North and South

By the end of 1861 the long duration of the war was already causing concern to many citizens on each side. By the end of 1862 its scale and cost had become matters of widespread dismay, not just in themselves, but also through their effects on both cherished institutions and on the familiar pattern of life.

The impact was naturally felt strongest in the South, since the war was in part a frontal assault on the slave economy there and all that entailed. Union representatives repeatedly attempted to provoke a slave rising or slave desertions in southern territory, though they were rarely either very subtle or very successful. The 200,000 black troops raised for the US army at least constituted a potent symbol for the "men of color" on both sides, though the effect was somewhat neutralized by the shameful discrimination they suffered. They received only half the pay of white soldiers, and were normally relegated to menial laboring duties rather than being sent into battle. Tens of thousands of them would die of sickness and neglect, but only some 2,700 would fall to the enemy's fire. On the few occasions that they were allowed to face their tormentors in combat, they were almost always badly used, as in the Petersburg crater on July 30th 1864. This is not to mention the very special ferocity reserved for them and their white officers by the outraged Confederates.

By refusing to mobilize their three and a half million slaves for the army until November 1864, when it was far too late, white Confederate males accepted a far heavier military burden than they might otherwise have had to. After allowance has been made for divided loyalties in the border states, they furnished almost a million soldiers out of an available white population of around six million. This compares with just under two million Union soldiers drawn from a population of twenty-one million. Hence the southerners were just under twice as likely to end up in the ranks, once there, to become casualties. Their civilian brothers also paid twice as much tax as northerners. Admittedly part of the war's burden could be met by using slaves to dig trenches and work on the lines of communications, but the North could employ its own freed or runaway slaves to do the same for little more than a slave's wages.

Perhaps still more subversive for the Confederacy were the strains placed upon states' and individuals' rights by the needs of war. Because the original argument for secession had been put forward in terms of defending these rights against federal interference, it was difficult now to impose a new centralizing federal authority, even if this originated from Richmond not Washington. The Confederate constitution of March 1861 had not spelt out the member states' continuing right to secede. It had instead talked of an intention to form a "permanent government," i.e. a newly binding federal power. Nevertheless the Richmond administration continued to act with great circumspection when it came to both states' rights and individuals rights. This was especially true of the Vice President, Alexander H. Stephens of Georgia, who was far more doctrinaire on the issue than President Davis. The latter was acutely aware of the need to change established customs and introduce centralized control in order to win the war, but Stephens was more aware of the principles for which the southern states had seceded in the first place.

The free-enterprise independence, if not anarchy, of the railroad companies made the most notorious case in point, since the Richmond government could never bring itself to nationalize and regulate them to the extent the war demanded. As a result the armies received a haphazard service from a railroad that was fragmented into something like 120 different companies. Each of these worked to its own time meridian, using its own choice of at least four different track gauges, and often not deigning to connect their rails to those of their competitors. On even quite short journeys, therefore, military stores might have to be unloaded at one station and carted a few miles across town to the station of some other company. The timetables would not, of course, be synchronized to allow for this, and equally might in any case decide to give precedence to a shipment of luxury goods for a private citizen, instead.

If railroads made the prime showcase for the military inefficiencies caused by "southern rights', it was far from difficult to find other examples. Soldiers, guns, rations, telegraph wire, indeed absolutely any commodity of military importance that anyone could possibly think of, all fell within the sphere of potential clashes between state and federal authorities. One state might interpret the conscription rules in such a way as to protect its sons from the draft. Another might bid against the Richmond government when buying rifles on the European arms market. A third state might distribute cheap food to the poor while the army went hungry. Union General William T. Sherman at one point even believed the state of Georgia was so far estranged from the Davis administration that it might make a separate peace.

Such problems were further aggravated by the very personal nature of southern politics. Neither Davis nor his opponents based their power on anything like a modern party machine. Instead, they operated as individuals, each serving what they personally understood to be Confederate ideology. Every measure that came up for discussion had therefore to be considered according to the different ways in which a large number of individuals chose to view it, rather then according to some well- organized party programme. The result was that Davis had to do a great deal of his lobbying in person, and lacked the bureaucratic support that he so badly needed. His government worked in a very old-fashioned manner, in contrast to Lincoln's far more streamlined methods.

There were many ways in which the Confederacy was unfit to fight a modern total war, yet surprisingly it was actually quite successful in mobilizing its resources. Starting from practically nothing, the South constructed a makeshift arms industry that was almost adequate for its army's needs. By introducing conscription early on in the war, it admittedly created several types of draft-dodger, but it did ultimately get a very high proportion of southern manpower into the army. If it could not give them smart uniforms, boots or regular rations, it could at least dig them extensive trenchworks and provide both inspired leadership and strong esprit de corps. Towards the end of the war Davis was even able to seize, in the name of survival, strong centralized powers that seemed to go against everything the South was fighting for. His law of March 1863 for commandeering private property represented a major infringement of individual rights, and the final acceptance of blacks to the army was a still more radical capitulation.

In the North the strains of war were felt less acutely than in the South, and in many places normal everyday life prevailed. As in the South, it was widely felt that the war should not infringe on the freedom of politics or of the individuals, although these were interpreted in rather different ways. In the North there was less difficulty in asserting the president's constitutional wartime powers, whereby he was authorised to cut across some democratic freedoms in the interests of the common defense. Lincoln could, for example, bring a greater measure of federal control to the railroads and telegraph lines than was possible in the South. He even insisted on a much tighter supervision of his generals. On the other hand the Union saw continuing political debate as the essence of what it was fighting for, so all manner of critics had to be accepted, even when they were well organized in apparently subversive political parties.

Despite some censorship, investigations and arrests, there was certainly a far greater toleration of the anti-war movement than could have been conceivable in the South. The so-called "Copperheads" were radical members of the Democratic party, and were especially strong in the Midwest, but with support from many less extreme groups. Their influence was demonstrated by the high Democratic vote in the congressional elections of 1862, and in Indiana and Illinois the state legislatures even became so difficult to manage that their Republican governors took extra legal steps to bypass them. Anti-war feelings came to the boil the following year in protest against the Emancipation Proclamation, against martial law, and especially against the blatant inequalities of the March 1863 Conscription Act. Coinciding with Lee's invasion of Pennsylvania in July, the first attempt to apply this act provoked widespread unrest, and in New York City hundreds of people were killed in gigantic draft riots that soon turned into anti-black race riots. Thus did xenophobic support of the Union turn into xenophobic racial attacks that can only have given comfort to the Confederacy. Copperhead influence was to sink into the background only during the 1864 presidential campaign, when General McClellan, as both a soldier and the Democratic candidate, discovered that the national mood had swung in favour of finishing off the war rather than abandoning it.

Standing as the principled and patriotic war party, the Republicans and their assorted allies enjoyed a major political advantage right from the start of hostilities. This was especially true of the Radical Republican abolitionist wing which could exploit the extremism of wartime, whereas in more normal times it would have exerted little influence. Despite being led by a civilian who often disagreed with the army, and often suffered military defeats, the Republican Party convinced the electorate that it alone held the secret of victory. The party narrowly won the congressional elections of 1862, then carried the presidential contest of 1864 by an especially wide margin, winning a vast majority of the army's vote, which it took great care to deliver to the ballot boxes.

An important part of Republican success stemmed from the fact that Lincoln was a politician to his fingertips, one who knew how to keep his policies closely aligned with the evolving wishes of both the party and the nation. This process was especially visible over the vexed question of slavery during the first two years of the war. Whereas in 1860 most Republicans had been content to allow slavery to continue in those states that already had it, by the time Lincoln came to issue his Emancipation Proclamation, on September 22nd 1862, he had realized that he could go even further. Although there was not yet a majority in favor of abolition, even within the Republican Party, two years of war had undermined much of the potential opposition, at least outside the border states. Provided Lincoln could move carefully, and "sell" the measure on the grounds of its expediency towards winning the war and preserving the Union, he could win sufficient assent for the measure to stick. Nor was the Emancipation Proclamation itself as revolutionary as

THE CIVIL WAR

the abolitionists had wanted. It foresaw only a gradual abolition of slavery, and emphatically rejected the blacks' aspirations to be considered equal to whites. It also applied only to the slaves held by the Confederates as of January 1st 1863, thereby leaving those held by Union supporters unaffected.

Emancipation was a momentous act introduced quietly and subtly. It was introduced less for humanitarian reasons than to help the war effort by undermining the Confederate economy, helping to recruit blacks for the US army, and appeasing European opinion. Nevertheless, Lincoln was at heart a humanitarian, and surely knew that his proclamation would effectively ensure the complete abolition of slavery in the long term, even if he was painfully anxious not to spell that out in the short term. The Emancipation Proclamation was a piece of effective propaganda rather than a very binding legal document; yet when all is said and done it was still a remarkable political achievement by an embattled president.

Lincoln was a modern man, who knew how to organize a government as well as he knew how to read the pulse of his party. He included all his leading Republican rivals in the cabinet, consulted with them and delegated authority effectively to them in a way that Jefferson Davis could never quite manage. The administrative tasks were certainly formidable, since unlike the Confederacy the North could call on a wealth of resources that seemed to be limited only by the government's ability to harness them. When Edwin M. Stanton became Secretary of War in January 1862 he brought a powerful business mind to that office, and coordinated military policy through an efficient War Board. By organizing the operations of the military telegraph he soon also made himself an indispensable center of information, receiving up-to-date reports around the clock from every far-flung army commander. The Navy was in good hands with Gideon Welles and successfully underwent a massive expansion from forty-two ships to almost 700, not to mention the ambitious programs for armored boats and riverine flotillas. A still greater expansion occurred in the supply department under Quartermaster General Montgomery C. Meigs, whose bureau expanded from thirteen clerks to 600, spending some 300 million dollars per year instead of just 5 million dollars pre-war. A good half of northern industry was brought into the war effort, which may not sound a very great proportion by twentieth-century standards, but was prodigious at the time. The war gave an enormous boost to an already rapidly expanding economy, both at the time and in the postwar reconstruction period. It was a boost after which the re-United States of America would never need to look back.

THE TIDE TURNS, 1863

The Gettysburg Campaign

In the summer of 1863 the Union faced an immediate crisis when General Lee advanced west and north out of his defences on the Rappahannock. Ably screening his movement with rear guard troops moved through the Shenandoah valley, across the Potomac and into Maryland and Pennsylvania. A strong Union reconnaissance was held off by J. E. B. Stuart and his men in the all-cavalry Battle of Brandy Station on June 9th. Despite suffering an initial surprise, the confederates got the better of the fight and found that the saber still had a place alongside the revolver and the carbine.

By June 24th the bulk of the Army of Northern Virginia was established in rich foraging ground in the Cumberland valley a hundred miles northwest from Washington. The Army of the Potomac was only just starting to cross into Maryland, in the direction of Frederick, and Lee was confident he had time to spread out and collect supplies before there was any danger of a battle. He was uncertain of the true position, however, since Stuart had taken the bulk of the cavalry off on a raid behind Union lines. Although this did cause some disruption to Meade's supply trains, the cavalry might have been better employed acting as the "eyes" of the Confederate commander. By June 30th the cavalry vanguard of the Union force was already north of Gettysburg, before southern troops were fully aware of the threat.

Thus the great battle of Gettysburg started somewhat accidentally the following morning as troops under General A. P. Hill tried to forage shoes in the town – but ran into Brigadier John Buford's thin screen of dismounted horsemen instead. In the ensuing fight the Confederates found they could make little progress, and both sides summoned reinforcements to the spot. By the afternoon the two armies were busy concentrating their whole force at Gettysburg, and each already had two complete army corps in position. After heavy fighting the northern troops evacuated the town itself, but took up defensive positions on rising ground just to the south – on Culp's Hill, Cemetery Hill and Cemetery Ridge. By nightfall on July 1st 1863 Confederate probing of these positions had found them to be very strong, and a number of senior commanders counseled against attacking them frontally.

Overnight, both sides prepared for a formal battle. Meade arrived and consolidated the defense, issuing strict orders against men who might be tempted to leave the ranks or disobey orders. Perhaps due to so many Union failures in the past this time when the whole course of the war apparently hung in the balance, Meade seems to have been pessimistic of the outcome. Lee held a much better tactical position than he had at Antietam, and had advanced much deeper into Union territory. If he defeated the Army of the Potomac he could rampage far and wide in the north, and perhaps cut off Washington itself. The Confederacy would thus win the overall initiative at last, with European recognition as a likely prize. Meade was therefore in no mood to take chances or to try risky attacks. When he later found that General Daniel E. Sickles had exceeded his orders by deploying his corps in a peach orchard almost a mile ahead of the main battle line, he was furious.

On the Confederate side, however, there was a seeming lack of the urgency and decisiveness that had characterized earlier battles. Lee advised an attack, but his lieutenants wanted to dig in on the defensive. Their men were weary and the enemy was strong; they made only half-hearted attempts to comply with Lee's wishes. Finally, Longstreet was ordered to outflank the Union line to the south, but it was only at 3 p.m. on July 2nd that he eventually opened fire. It may be speculated that by this time Stonewall Jackson, had he survived, might already have been trampling over Meade's baggage and attacking his headquarters from the rear.

In the event Longstreet won a partial victory, chasing off Sickles' overextended troops, and bringing acute pressure to bear against the open Union flank at the signal station on Little Round Top. He *almost* succeeded in seizing this key to the battlefield but was stymied in the nick of time by Brigadier Gouverneur K. Warren, the chief engineer responsible for signals who would later rise to command an army corps. By the end of the day both the Round Tops had been secured against the Confederates, while belated attacks against Culp's Hill on the northeastern flank of the Union line had also been beaten off. Meade's position was holding, but his intense trepidation remained. He almost decided to retreat overnight, but his subordinates dissuaded him.

Luckily for the Union, on July 3rd Lee uncharacteristically ran out of ideas. Failing to explore Longstreet's proposal of making a wider outflanking move to the south, he was aware only of his army's vulnerability and shortage of rations. He knew he could not stay much longer around Gettysburg, and any maneuver might lay him open to a destructive counter-attack. To cut through his dilemma, therefore, he determined to launch a massed frontal assault on the center of the Union line. His hope was that this Napoleonic "act of decision" would produce as great a victory as had those of the late French emperor. By selecting a wide bare field for the assault, however, he exposed his men to especially heavy fire that could not be suppressed, even by two and a half hours' artillery bombardment.

The attack, known as "Pickett's Charge" after its foremost commander, was launched around 2.30 p.m. and was greeted almost as soon as it broke out of the tree line on Seminary Ridge, by the converging fire of some two hundred cannon. This defense had been carefully husbanded by General Henry Hunt who had arranged something very similar at Malvern Hill a year earlier. Once within close range Pickett's men came under devastating infantry fire, and although some succeeded in reaching the Union trenches, they could not stay there. The attack melted away, and with it Lee's hope of reaping permanent gains from his invasion. He did not immediately concede defeat, however, but held his ground throughout the next day, vainly daring Meade to show some initiative. Then he slipped away unmolested, and a few days later was even allowed to build a bridge and cross the Potomac at Williamsport while the crushingly superior Union army looked passively on. In the battle the Union had suffered some 23,000 casualties, but they could still field 85,000 men. The Confederates, by contrast, had surely lost several thousand more men than the 20,000 they claimed, and at Williamsport they could muster barely 35,000 troops.

After the Gettysburg Campaign there was to be almost a year's "shadow boxing" in Virginia, without any general action until Grant tried to break the deadlock in May 1864. From this point of view Gettysburg can be seen as having altered little, even though it was certainly the biggest and most costly battle of the war. It was not a decisive battle in the sense of having disarmed the Confederacy, but it had demonstrated the North could still beat off invasion. Indeed, it took some time for the Union to appreciate the full extent of its victory. Perhaps it was only with Lincoln's Gettysburg Address on November 19th that the battle began to take on the epic and momentous renown that it has enjoyed ever since.

From a technical military point of view the Virginia maneuvers in the second half of 1863 were fascinating. First Lee, pursued by Meade, reoccuopied the old Rappahannock line. Then Meade outsmarted him in a daring thrust to Manassas in October, although there was to be no third battle there. A month later Meade turned Lee's position from the east, nearly fighting a new battle of Chancellorsville; but at Mine Run on November 30th Meade once again failed to launch a general assault, despite his continuing numerical superiority of almost two to one. Both sides finally came to rest, in winter quarters, on very much the same ground they had occupied for most of the war to date.

The Vicksburg Campaign

Meanwhile, during the first half of 1863 the focus of attention in the west had been Vicksburg, the Confederate bastion dominating the central Mississippi from its eastern bank. Grant had tried to start the siege by sending forward Sherman's corps in December the previous year, but four days after Christmas this had been repulsed at Chickasaw Bluffs, to the north of the city. General John A. McClernand then took command but allowed himself to be sidetracked by the lure of irrelevant glory on the Arkansas River, and it was not until Grant himself arrived at the end of January 1863 that the pressure on Vicksburg was resumed. All efforts to approach it either over land or via the inadequate secondary waterways, however, were failures. A canal to bypass the town to the west was even started, but had to be abandoned. Only in April, employing a complex plan scarcely less promising than any of its predecessors, did Grant finally manage to find his foothold. He distracted Confederate attention with a long, epoch-making cavalry raid around their rearguard, under General Benjamin H. Grierson. The main river fleet was then run down the Mississippi under the guns of the fortress, while Grant himself laid roads through difficult swampland and eventually brought 40,000 men, supported by lighter boats, in a wide swing around to the west. He then crossed the Mississippi thirty miles below Vicksburg and set out to encircle it from south and east.

Grant's logistic problem was so acute that he decided to cut loose from his uncertain supply line and advance deeper into Mississippi, living off the land. This would become a favorite technique of Sherman and Grant during the remainder of the war, although it was never a risk to be undertaken lightly. At least the technique negated Confederate attempts to cut Grant's line of communication, while giving his men an unexpected spur; if they wanted to eat, they had to keep moving. This they did in grand style, first seizing the rail junction at Jackson and then turning back, in a dazzling reversal, to assail General John C. Pemberton's force of 21,000 men advancing out of Vicksburg. Grant thrashed them at Champion's Hill on May 16th, and three days later was investing the city with normal supply lines reopened by the river fleet.

Attempts to assault the Vicksburg fortifications were uniformly unsuccessful, but Pemberton could neither break out nor replenish his food stocks. J. E. Johnston's attempted relief – too little and too late – melted away. The garrison was reduced to surrender by starvation on a bitterly resented July 4th, the day after Gettysburg had been lost. Grant had sustained some 10,000 casualties in the campaign, but had won his most spectacular prize.

Henceforth, and with the fall of Port Hudson on July 9th, the Confederacy was split in two. Its problems were still further intensified by Union advances in Tennessee, where Rosecrans finally got moving on June 26th. With a skilful feint to the west he marched his main body over difficult roads to the east, and turned Bragg out of the camps he had occupied since the battle of Murfreesboro. There was a pause while the displaced Bragg occupied the line of the Tennessee River, especially at the key rail center of Chattanooga. Then Rosecrans repeated his trick, starting on August 16th, and this time feinting to the east but making the main move to the west. Bragg evacuated Chattanooga, thereby abandoning a major defense line and depriving the Confederacy of a vital east-west rail route.

THE CIVIL WAR

By September 10th on Chickamauga Creek, however, Bragg had recovered his poise sufficiently to have his army more centrally concentrated than his opponent's. For several days the two sides probed, maneuvered and skirmished, with the Confederates missing some excellent opportunities to defeat the Union forces piecemeal. Then, on September 18th, Longstreet's corps from the Army of Northern Virginia began to arrive, giving the South a rare parity with a Union army. Bragg took the decision to unleash the whole force into the attack. The battle started the next day, but the Confederates made little progress until Longstreet himself entered the fray late in the morning of September 20th. He chanced to find a gap in the enemy line and pushed through it, causing widespread dismay. Rosecrans believed the battle was lost, and retreated, but Bragg failed to switch his reserves fast enough to exploit this opporunity. General George H. Thomas stood firm on the battlefield in a well-fortified position, earning his nickname of "the rock of Chickamauga" and denying the Confederates many of the fruits of victory. Overall they sustained nearly 19,000 casualties as opposed to 16,000 from the Union side, although they did at least secure a rich haul of much-needed muskets and cannon.

After Chickamauga, Bragg followed Rosecrans back to Chattanooga, partially invested it, but could not take it. Perched on Missionary Ridge overlooking the town, Bragg suffered from an overstretched supply line and an army that his severe discipline had driven close to mutiny. He despatched Longstreet on an abortive campaign against Knoxville, Tennessee. Although this eased his supply problem it only weakened him in the face of an increasing Union build-up, and made a poor end to a campaign that sometimes promised much better things.

The Anaconda Comes of Age

The fall of Vicksburg had finally thrown the Confederates off the Mississippi; the loss of Chattanooga and Knoxville had thrown them off the Tennessee, and Gettysburg had thrown them off the Potomac. During the final eighteen months of the war they would be beleaguered in an ever-shrinking circle, increasingly deprived of the wherewithal for making war, and with ever-diminishing freedom of action.

Around the coasts the vise was being remorselessly tightened. The loss of Fort Sumter in Charleston harbor was a symbol that continued to rankle with the Union, and a campaign to reverse that loss was started in April 1863. At first naval bombardments were tried, but these failed, even when nine ironclads were used. Next, troops were landed at nearby Fort Wagner, where a costly but eventually successful siege ensued. Sumter could then be battered by guns sited on land, but its island location and powerful secondary fortifications, booms and mines protected it from direct attack. The next year the defenders of Charleston even sank a ship in the blockading fleet with a kamikaze submarine attack. It was not until in February 1865 that the defiant stronghold would finally be retaken by Sherman, approaching from inland.

In late 1863 there were many other new Union blockading operations, albeit far from uniformly successful. Garrisons were established in Arkansas and on the Texan border with Mexico, but the bombardment of Fort McAllister near Savannah, Georgia, proved in vain. The following year Jacksonville in Florida was captured, but the troops were prevented by the Confederates from advancing any further inland. At Fort Fisher near Wilmington, North Carolina, the garrison gallantly held out under Butler's land and sea attack. Banks' ill-starred Red River expedition in Louisiana met a still more humiliating reverse. In Plymouth, North Carolina, there was even a well coordinated southern assault that recaptured territory previously taken by the Union. However an innovative attack by a US

torpedo boat there would later sink the southern ironclad *Albemarle.*

By far the most spectacular coastal operation of this period, however, was Farragut's capture of the defences of Mobile on August 5th 1864. Steaming past the forts at the mouth of the river, he reacted decisively when his fleet was held up by a boom and one of the monitors was sunk by a mine. Uttering the immortal phrase "Damn the torpedoes! Full speed ahead!," Farragut urged the whole force forward through the obstacles and emerged unscathed on the far side. He was unable to capture the city itself, but he destroyed the Confederate ships at anchor there and completely closed the vitally important harbor to commerce.

In support of these operations the Union found it had to execute a legal and diplomatic "about face" on many of the questions raised by blockading, and could no longer pose as a champion of freedom on the seas. The 1848 treaty with Mexico, for example, had expressly forbidden a blockade of the Rio Grande. Something very close to one had however been imposed on Matamoros, the Mexican port on the Rio Grande that was a busy center for traffic going to the Confederacy. Equally, before 1861, the USA had usually opposed the activities of blockading navies, such as the British in 1812. The Civil War had scarcely started, however, before the northern fleet was taking Confederates off neutral ships, or impounding the ships themselves for trading with the South. This caused a number of diplomatic incidents, especially with Britain, and it was only by the exercise of considerable tact, diplomacy and prevarication that international harmony could be maintained.

Very similar qualities were needed to hamper the activities of Confederate commerce raiders, many of which were built in Europe and frequented neutral harbors. These fast, well-armed warships caused great nuisance by roaming far and wide across the world's oceans, sinking Union shipping wherever it was found. The CSS *Florida* was only destroyed by an attack that violated Brazilian waters and neutrality. The CSS *Shenandoah* chased Union whalers as far afield as the Bering Straits, and it survived the war. Most successful of all was the CSS *Alabama,* which escaped from under the noses of Federal agents in Liverpool, England, to wreak havoc on the sea lanes until finally run to earth and sunk off Cherbourg, France, on June 19th 1864.

The commerce raiders effectively chased the American flag off the North Atlantic route, although they could not blockade northern ports or stop trade conducted by neutrals. This could only have happened if the Confederacy had managed to build more and more powerful ships, which was something the Federal agents in Europe worked hard to prevent. When the *Florida* and the *Alabama* were first launched from British slipways the Union was caught off guard, but it soon regained its poise and mounted a devastating diplomatic and legal offensive throughout Europe. This succeeded in destroying the nascent Confederate Navy at source. In 1863 the USA almost threatened war with Britain unless she prevented the launching of two powerful ironclad rams that were being built in Liverpool. They were bought instead by the Royal Navy, and an even bigger warship being built in Glasgow was diverted from the Confederacy to Denmark. Something similar happened to six warships that had been ordered in France, although one of them was later bought back from Denmark by the Confederates, in American waters only to arrive a month after the war ended.

By 1864 the naval northern blockade had already taken a terrible toll on the southern war economy, but it was now joined by a second powerful economic weapon. This was the systematic Union use of overland raiding, an altogether more controversial and legally dubious process then even the widespread interruption of maritime trade. Overland raiding was General Grant's selected policy when neither direct battle nor the original Anaconda Plan seemed to offer a definite end to hostilities. More than anything else, perhaps, it has come to symbolize the unconventional and less humane strategies employed as the Civil War entered its fourth and last debilitating year.

There was nothing particularly new about raiding, despite recent claims for its novelty made by recent historians. Students of European warfare would recognise it as a classic, if not *the* classic method, of exerting pressure on an enemy, in use from medieval times or even earlier. The aim was not to capture or to occupy territory, but to move rapidly through it living off the land and laying waste the enemy's assets along the way. By demonstrating that a man was powerless to protect his own crops, cattle and industries, one might discredit his government in his eyes, and those of his fellow men, and thereby persuade him to accept terms. The raiding army would also be relieved of the burden of logistics, since it would be making the war pay for itself.

By the 1860s the raiding system had largely fallen out of use among civilized nations, having been replaced by more "strategic" strikes to seize territory or destroy an enemy's field army. The tactic was therefore viewed with widespread suspicion when it was re-introduced in the Civil War not merely by its innocent civilian victims, but also by military purists. Many modern commentators have also called it militarily irrelevant and have dismissed it, for example, merely as a "favorite – and generally profitless – practice." Because they took forces away from the potentially decisive battlefield, the raiders could be accused not just of cruelty to civilians, but of weakening the chances for a quick end to the war. Yet there has always been a "pro-raiding" lobby, prepared to see it as a necessary and innovative technique of economic warfare. With all the justification of hindsight, too, it has been hailed as prefiguring the strategic bombing campaigns of the twentieth century.

The whole issue came to the fore when General Grant took command of the army which was stuck in Chattanooga, and was apparently powerless to break through the encircling Confederate trenches on Missionary Ridge. Grant saw the difficulty of assaulting the enemy on the battlefield, just as he understood the difficulty of keeping open his long supply line. He was only too well aware of its vulnerability to Confederate raiding, not least because he had dabbled in raiding himself, at the time of his Vicksburg maneuvers. It was therefore only a logical step for him to think of mounting bigger and better raids in future; raids that could bypass the difficulties of the battlefield at the same time as they solved the problems of supply. From this time onwards Grant planned a series of fast operations deep into the heart of the Confederacy, using infantry and artillery as well as cavalry. Naturally he shared these ideas with his subordinates, not least General Sherman. There were to be a number of delays and distractions before the concept could be properly put into practice, but for the rest of the war the "big raid" strategy was securely established as the goal to be aimed at before any other.

NEW STRATEGIES, NEW HORIZONS

From Chattanooga to Atlanta and the Sea

The immediate task facing Grant at Chattanooga was to break out of the Confederate siege and regain mobility. This he did in grand style, first capturing Lookout Mountain in "the battle above the clouds" on November 24th 1863, then turning to assault the apparently formidable Missionary Ridge next day. Amazingly, the defense of this steep and heavily fortified position collapsed like a house of cards. Whether it was because they were starving, or demoralized by Bragg's harsh discipline, or simply because their trenches had been dug in the wrong places, the Confederates seemed to lack their customary tenacity. When their first skirmish line broke at the foot of the hill, the fugitives from it retreated up the slope and blocked the fields of fire of the men higher up. Seizing their chance, the Union attackers pushed on and over succeeding trenches. Bragg's army dissolved in one of the most sudden and unexpected panics of the war, suffering some 6,700 killed, wounded or taken prisoner. This was doubly remarkable for a defending force, since casualties were almost a thousand more than those suffered by the more exposed attackers.

The armies came to rest for the winter some twenty miles to the southeast of Chattanooga. Here the Confederates occupied Rocky Face Ridge, covering Dalton and the railroad to Atlanta. Bragg was replaced by J. E. Johnston, while Grant was called to Washington to take overall command of the Union armies. His successor in the west was Sherman, whose painstaking style left nothing to chance, either in logistics or in outflanking the enemy under the cover of feint movements.

The advance on Atlanta was resumed on May 7th 1864, with a series of flanking maneuvers around the western end of Johnston's line. The latter was acutely conscious that he was outnumbered by at least three to two, and that the southern manpower pool had all but dried up. He was therefore anxious not to risk costly battles, since he would be unable to replace casualties. Instead, he preferred to withdraw each time, rather than fight. He also tried to spare his men by digging them in at every possible opportunity. It was perhaps in this campaign then that the spade was used more than in any other before 1915. The Confederates would occupy complex trenchworks wherever they stopped, and Sherman's men would fortify their own lines opposite, to match. The two armies would then face each other for a few days while Sherman collected his supplies, then a new flanking move would drive Johnston back to his next chosen line. Sometimes he would have two or three such lines prepared in advance by gangs of slaves, so his army would simply have to step back a couple of miles when the pressure began to tell, and would be immediately and fully protected.

Despite his superior numbers, Sherman was also reluctant to risk his men's lives by making frontal assaults. Besides, when he had tried that approach at Chickasaw Bluffs he had been defeated. Even in the generally successful offensive at Chattanooga his own immediate command had been held up by enemy defenses. He therefore now preferred to play along with Johnston's relatively bloodless game of digging and marching, rarely involving any actual fighting. His men satisfied their honor by loosing off plenty of ammunition in the skirmish line, but if they could keep advancing without closer combat than that, everyone was happy. Only once did Sherman order a massed frontal assault, at Kenesaw Mountain on June 27th. As he probably feared, this led merely to a bloody repulse, although with 3,000 casualties it was considerably less bloody than many of the other "slaughter pens" of the Civil War.

About the only people who were unhappy with this stately minuet being danced by Sherman and Johnston were to be found in the Confederate high command. The nearer the battle line approached to

THE CIVIL WAR

the key industrial city of Atlanta, the more worrying the situation became. Eventually Johnston's apparent led to his replacement by a man who could certainly not be accused of passivity, General John B Hood. Hood had caused heavy casualties among his men by leading assaults at Gaines' Mill, Second Manassas, Antietam, Gettysburg, where he had lost the use of an arm, and Chickamauga, where he had lost a leg. Now he reversed Johnston's cautious policy in a most spectacular, if quickly disastrous, manner. He launched three frontal assaults between July 20th and 28th, at Peachtree Creek, Atlanta and Ezra Church. All were repulsed, and Hood sustained a total of some 19,000 casualties, a third of his army. Thereafter he was thrown on the defensive in Atlanta until this was turned by the last of Sherman's wide hooks round to the west. The city was evacuated and Union forces entered it on September 2nd.

Hood had lost the campaign, though it is doubtful that Johnston could have saved it. Being the irrepressible battler he was, however, Hood now determined to seize the initiative and win a new campaign based on daring and rapid movement. In October he started north up Sherman's railroad to Chattanooga, but found he could inflict little damage that could not quickly be repaired. Avoiding Chattanooga, therefore, he moved west to cross the Tennessee at Florence, then thrust north towards Nashville. Once this would have led Sherman to abandon his prize at Atlanta and join the pursuit, but by this stage in the war he was not to be drawn. He knew that Thomas held a powerful army around Nashville, and could be trusted to defend it from attack. For his own part he was preparing to launch the great march to the sea that would devastate the Confederacy from one end to the other.

Hood reached Franklin on November 30th. Where his costly assaults on an outnumbered Union defense were unable to break through. No less than a dozen Confederate generals were hit in this battle, including five killed, and they could not stop the Union concentrating over 55,000 men at Nashville itself. When he arrived outside the town Hood had less than half that number, and when Thomas finally sallied forth on December 15th, the result was really a foregone conclusion. The Confederates fought hard for two days, but were overwhelmed. A horrific retreat in terrible weather ensued, and Hood's army all but ceased to exist. By March 1865 Thomas was able to send his powerful cavalry corps, under General James H. Wilson, on a big raid through Alabama to Selma, doing much the same job there as Sherman was already doing in Georgia and the Carolinas.

Sherman's march had begun on November 15th 1864, leaving Atlanta burnt and its industries entirely destroyed. Northern apologists have attempted to show that he had intended only limited destructions of key Confederate property, but by starting in the business of destruction at all, he must surely have known it was likely to run out of control. The same was true of his 60,000-strong army's movement across country, spread out on a fifty-mile frontage like some vast swarm of blue locusts. Uncontrolled foragers, or "bummers," visited every house, forcibly taking all the food the army needed and destroying the rest. Money and valuables might also be "requisitioned," and still heavier penalties inflicted on identified Confederate activists. The railroad tracks were torn up, heated and twisted into unusable loops, nicknamed "Sherman's neckties" while the towns along the way, such as Columbia, South Carolina, were burned. This is clearly what Sherman later meant when he said that "all war is all hell," although he seems to have been relatively little troubled by his own personal rôle as presiding devil.

There was only a pitifully small force of Confederates, under Beauregard, Hardee and finally J. E. Johnston, to contest this advance - and they were always kept guessing as to where Sherman's men would move next. First the Union troops went to Savannah and linked up with the fleet, capturing Fort McAllister on December 13th, and the port itself

on December 21st. The news caused a sensation in the North, since the policy of raiding had implied a severance not only of the army's line of communication, but also of its regular reporting to Washington. Sherman had thus emerged triumphant, not merely from the enemy's heartland, but also from a news blackout that many had feared concealed a disaster. After resting a month or so the army continued its devastations into South and then North Carolina, joining with another Union force from Fort Fisher and Wilmington on the way. Whenever Johnston stood and tried to fight it out, as at Bentonville on March 19th 1865, he could soon be overpowered by a concentration of superior numbers.

Mobile also fell in March, to yet another Union column, underlining the lesson that the South had now finally run out of armies. Northern troops could roam freely wherever they wished, and, barring systematic guerrilla warfare, they could not be opposed. The guerrilla warfare option was deliberately renounced, however, since it would merely have protracted the suffering without serving any useful purpose. Johnston therefore sought an armistice and engaged in a dialogue with his opponent. Sherman, in what he admirably took to be the late President Lincoln's spirit of reconciliation; at first exceeded his authority; he wanted to grant more lenient terms than his government actually wished. He was reprimanded for this but, eventually, a formal surrender was mutually agreed on April 26th 1865 at Greensboro, North Carolina. The area west of the Mississippi would be surrendered precisely one month later.

From the Wilderness to Petersburg

Thus the war came to an end in the western theater. It had seen the raiding system perfected by Sherman during his march, by Wilson in his Alabama campaign, and by a number of lesser raiders elsewhere. The same system was also tried in Virginia, but there it always remained a secondary weapon. When Grant took command in the spring of 1864 he hoped that victory in the east would be won on the battlefield instead.

Grant's campaign began on May 3rd, just a few days before Sherman started moving towards Atlanta. The Army of the Potomac crossed the Rapidan and entered the Wilderness around the old Chancellorsville battle site. Lee was not slow to observe this move, and his forces were soon marching up from their camps further to the west to intercept. They made contact on May 5th near the Wilderness tavern, before the cumbersome Union trains had cleared the densely-wooded area. There was a vicious two-day battle in which neither side could make an impression on the other, despite some 16,000 Union and 11,000 Confederate casualties. Longstreet was wounded, in circumstances similar to Jackson's fall near the same spot, which cast a long shadow over southern operations. When forest fires engulfed the casualties where they lay, it added yet another element of horror to the already fearsome event.

Grant's next move was to start a series of outflanking maneuvers very similar to Sherman's between Chattanooga and Atlanta, although this time the Union troops moved around their enemy's eastern flank, rather than the Western. Another crucial difference was that Grant, unlike Sherman, seemed less reluctant to launch frontal assaults. He wanted to destroy Lee's army as well as to hustle it southwards, and when it became clear that this would not be possible, he devised yet another novel strategy to justify his costly attacks. In a word, he embraced a strategy of "attrition," whereby fierce combat was welcomed in the interests of increasing the mutual losses to both combatants.

Grant knew that the South was desperately short of manpower, whereas the North was more than amply supplied with troops. If both sides lost heavily in frequent battles, therefore, the South would eventually run out completely, leaving the Union triumphant. The Wilderness campaign thus represented a deliberate attempt to provoke a series of frequent and costly battles. The same economics extended to the policy of exchanging prisoners, which had applied up to that point. Grant saw it merely as a way of giving back good soldiers to the Confederacy after they had once been lost in combat. He therefore forbade exchanges of prisoners; every man captured would now remain out of action until the end of the war. As a practical exercise in simple logic this doctrine cannot easily be faulted, although unfortunately it threw an unexpectedly heavy strain on both sides' prisoner of war camps. These were ill-equipped to deal with anything more than low, transient populations of prisoners. The high, permanent populations that they now housed overtaxed the available rations, sanitation and the goodwill of the guards. The rate of deaths in captivity soared upwards into tens of thousands, due to neglect, a variety of diseases and assault. Although this was also true of Union prisons, it was most prevelent in those of the beleaguered Confederacy. Libby Prison, Richmond, was bad enough; but still worse was that at Andersonville, Georgia, ironically built to relieve it. Out of 34,000 inmates, 13,000 died, amid scenes only too indicative of the concentration camps to emerge in more recent times.

After the battle of the Wilderness Grant's attrition policy brought him to a new battle, at Spottsylvania. Poor screening by the cavalry and hard marching by the Confederates had allowed Lee to set up a strong defensive position across the army's path. This Grant duly attacked, starting on May 10th. Fighting became fiercest around the "Mule Shoe" salient. Colonel Emory Upton organized and executed a model attack that went a long way towards disproving the supposed invincibility of Civil War field fortifications, but he was left unsupported and eventually had to retire. On May 12th Hancock's corps repeated the exploit, though they fell into disarray and were finally held off. During the next week Grant tried again to find an open flank. He abandoned his quest, however, on May 20th, in favor of a wide swing to the southeast – in an attempt to reach the North Anna river before his opponent. At Spottsylvania he had suffered some 17,000 casualties as against only 10,000 from the Confederate side.

Meanwhile Grant had extended the raiding process to the eastern theater. General Philip H. Sheridan's cavalry corps was sent out towards Richmond to chase off the Confederate cavalry and destroy railroads. At Yellow Tavern on May 11th they successfully dispersed Stuart's cavalry. Although they mortally wounded him, they could not penetrate the Richmond defenses and eventually withdrew. At the same time two other Union detachments were encountering difficulties on the further flanks. In the Shenandoah valley the first of three Union campaigns was turned back at New Market on May 15th, a battle made famous by the exemplary comportment of the cadets of the Virginia Military Institute. Similarly, to the southeast of Richmond, a large force under Butler advanced up the James River but was halted by inferior numbers at Drewry's Bluff. The force withdrew to Bermuda Hundred where it dug in and waited for the situation to improve. This supine inactivity wasted an excellent chance of capturing the Confederate capital, or at least of diverting large forces away from Lee's army.

At the battle of The North Anna Grant again found himself facing a line of fieldworks, and again realised their full extent only too late. Despite several desperate local combats between May 23rd and 26th, he decided against a general assault and set off again on more flank marches through poor weather and on bad roads. By June 3rd his army was almost in sight of Richmond, ready to attack at Cold Harbor on the old Gaines' Mill battlefield of 1862. Unfortunately the attack was launched unreconnoitered and too late. The Confederates were ready and waiting, and the result was one of the worst "slaughter pens" of the war. Some 7,000 Union casualties were sustained within the space of just a few minutes, as against a mere 1,500 Confederate casualties. If this was attrition, the sort of attrition that the Confederates could accept.

After the assault on Cold Harbor the two armies dug in and watched each other. Then, in the middle of June, Grant pulled off the most masterly of all his outflanking maneuvers. Quietly evacuating their trench lines, his men marched east, then south to the James River. Covered by light rear guards they successfully blinded Lee to their intentions. On the James itself a remarkable bridge was built, over a third of a mile long, and by June 16th the whole army had crossed to the southern shore. From here it could advance to relieve the besieged Butler, and advance on the lightly defended Petersburg, then emerge north of that city to assail Richmond from the rear.

Unfortunately for Grant, the initial attack on Petersburg, between June 15th and 18th, was badly bungled. After their experiences between the Wilderness and Cold Harbor, the Union forces were reluctant to press home frontal assaults. They failed to capture the city while it lay at their mercy, and this gave for Lee's army time to arrive and stabilize the situation by June 22nd. Trench warfare ensued, which allowed both armies a much-deserved rest, but failed to bring the end of the war any nearer. When a major assault was attempted in conjunction with a massive mine, at the battle of the crater on July 30th, weeks of careful preparation were thrown away by a last-minute change of plan. The black division that had prepared for the assault was stood down for political reasons and replaced by a quite unprepared white one. This and two other divisions failed to exploit the wide gap in Confederate defenses created by the mine, and the black troops had to be sent in after all. Alas, they arrived too late. The Confederates had consolidated their defense and were shooting down the attackers by the score. Altogether some 4,400 Union casualties were sustained in this battle; one that had come so close to cutting through to Richmond and victory. After it, Grant finally abandoned the idea of making frontal assaults, and contented himself with extending the trench lines ever further to the west. By the end of October, in front of Petersburg alone, the Confederate lines were already some twelve miles long. Five months later the whole line, including the Richmond defenses, would stretch no less than 53 miles.

While the two armies were settling down to the Petersburg siege, a second Union raid down the Shenandoah Valley was being seen off at Lynchburg. Lee sent the army corps of General Jubal A. Early to meet it. He pursued it north to the Potomac, crossed that river and, by July 11th, was in sight of Washington itself. With his small, tired force, however, he could not hope to storm the capital's defenses, and he pulled back to the Shenandoah. Once there, he found that his diversionary maneuver had been only too successful in attracting strong Union forces away from the Richmond area. General Sheridan now arrived to coordinate a crushing riposte. In a campaign that combined decisive combat with a systematic scorched earth policy, Sheridan beat Early in battles at Winchester and Cedar Creek on September 19th and October 19th respectively. In the meantime he stripped the valley of supplies, and allowed Grant to boast that if a crow wanted to fly across the area, it would have to take along its own rations. It was to be a bleak winter indeed for the Confederacy.

THE CIVIL WAR

The Appomattox Campaign

The final convulsions of the war in Virginia began when Lee made a last desperate surprise attack. Now promoted to the new post of commander in chief of all Confederate armies he advanced upon Fort Stedman, to the east of Petersburg, on March 25th 1865. Initial success soon turned to failure, and the assault was beaten off. Since the new campaigning season had now opened, however, Grant set his own army in motion towards the Southside Railroad, the last supply line into Petersburg. This move again extended the line to the west, although by March 31st it had been stabilized on the White Oak Road.

On this occasion, the Union infantry and artillery was helped by a powerful new auxiliary – Sheridan's mobile spearhead of hard-hitting cavalry. Combat-hardened in the Shenandoah operations, they were now anxious to cooperate closely with the infantry. Grant had originally wanted to detach the cavalry for a more strategic raiding rôle far from the main army. Sheridan had insisted, however, that its best use would be to maintain momentum at the cutting edge of the army's flank marches. In this way Lee's counter-moves could be preempted in a way that had not been seen before and so, in the event, it turned out.

The start of the cavalry's campaign was not propitious, since Sheridan was surprised by Pickett at Dinwiddie Court House on March 31st. He soon recovered, however, and the following day pushed back the enemy at Five Forks. Even though his cooperation with Warren's infantry left much to be desired, Sheridan did maintain his momentum and pursued the enemy across the vital Southside Railroad. Warren himself was unfairly sacked for his pains. So overstretched and unbalanced were the Confederates after this that a major offensive on April 2 along the White Oak Road won a rarely decisive breakthrough. The Confederates were pushed back six miles to the outskirts of Petersburg itself. Lee realized that his position there was hopeless, and overnight both the army and the government were pulled out of the whole Petersburg-Richmond area. The ten-month siege had ended in a Union victory.

Sheridan now took the lead in what became the most energetic pursuit of the war. Admittedly he was as much helped by Confederate exhaustion, straggling, and logistic weaknesses, as by the overwhelming numerical odds in favor of the northern side. It would be churlish, even so, to deny the part played by his own personal brand fiery leadership, combined with his innovative concept of spearheading operations using a self-contained cavalry force. By April 5th he was heading off Lee's army at Jetersville Station. The next day he rounded up a sizeable rear guard at Sayler's Creek. By April 8th he was across Lee's line of retreat at Appomattox Court House, having successfully outmarched him and traped him between two closing Union forces. On April 9th the Confederates failed to break out of the encirclement, and surrendered.

At Appomattox Lee decided against the option of continuing guerrilla warfare. He succeeded instead in winning free passage for his men to their homes – in effect a general amnesty that set a vital precedent. Although many individuals would be badly treated in the immediate aftermath of the war, there was to be no general witch hunt. Many of the opposing officers shook hands cordially at Appomattox, although there were still some exceptions, such as the Confederate General, Henry A. Wise. He refused to make a conciliatory gesture, crisply assuring one of his victors that "We hate you, sir."

The Final Reckoning

The most dramatic sequel to the Appomattox peace was the assassination of President Lincoln during a visit to the theater on the night of April 14th. John Wilkes Booth, a disgruntled Washington actor, had hatched a grandiose plot with some Confederate sympathisers simultaneously to murder several leading members of the government. Lincoln was obviously the prime target, especially as his unscathed survival through four years of war had made him unduly lax about his personal security. However, Vice President Johnson and Secretary of State Seward were also to be attacked. In the event Seward and his son did suffer severe knife wounds.

Booth's part in the conspiracy was to enter the presidential box, shoot Lincoln in the back of the head and then escape via the stage. This he fulfilled, unfortunately marring his theatrical exit by breaking his leg in the process. He was eventually tracked down by the authorities and killed while resisting arrest. Four of his co-conspirators were also arrested and executed, and others received long jail sentences. There were many hysterical demands to extend the blame to Jefferson Davis, or even to Lincoln's own Vice President and heir to his office, Andrew Johnson. Johnson was a war-Democrat from the South who held scarcely any common ground with the mainstream of northern Republican thinking. Nor, prior to the assassination, had anyone ever considered him to be presidential material he had only been there to balance the ticket. It was to be with acute dismay and suspicion, therefore, that many of Lincoln's supporters found themselves passing on the sacred trust to such an inappropriate successor. If the murder had occurred at a more critical point in the war, it is quite possible that the repercussions might have been far more ugly.

In effect Lincoln's death was similar to Franklin D. Roosevelt's, in that it did not lead to the collapse of national purpose that his enemies had hoped for. in a sense it can even be seen as a fitting end to a war in which he had himself been so much the central character. Lincoln certainly escaped President Wilson's fate in 1919, when the nation turned sharply against the victor's vision of a postwar world. The reverse side of this coin of course is that Lincoln was deprived of the chance to put his own vision into practice. If he had survived to do that, it is likely that his statesmanship would have gathered far more solid fruits from the victory than were actually secured.

If the Civil War was won by a "modern" political and economic mobilization, it seems that the peace was soon lost through the North's failure to adopt a modern political perspective. Naturally many of the victors hoped for a profound social change throughout the South. However, they had not seriously thought through the implications of this, and were unready to intervene actively on anything like the scale required. Where massive land grants for freed slaves were necessary, there was only a deep reluctance to interfere with existing private property. In view of their systematic wartime destruction of Confederate property in the interests of negro emancipation, this seems a strange, self-imposed restriction by northern politicians. Equally a sustained underpinning of black rights, by force if necessary, was essential if those rights were to become a reality. Yet in the event the army was speedily demobilized and by the early 1870s there were little more than 5,000 Federal troops remaining in the South. This was entirely inadequate to counter the Ku Klux Klan and the other racist paramilitary organizations campaigning to terrorize blacks into subservience. Yet in view of widespread northern racism, the political will that might have come to the defense of the former slaves was absent.

Much of the postwar northern leniency towards the South can be attributed to the new President, Andrew Johnson. He was soon found to be unequal to the task of reconciling conflicting viewpoints about the shape reconstruction should take. Indeed, he embraced a policy of reconciliation exclusively towards southern whites, and in many eyes appeared to be strongly pro-Confederate. He encouraged the defeated southern leaders to carry on from where they had left off, albeit without the right to secession or the theoretical right to own slaves. By means of amnesties and pardons he restored the same men to political power as had fought and lost the war. By leaving states free to make their own laws, he effectively excluded blacks from human or political rights, and in many cases even from the right to wages.

Johnson's policies immediately plunged the nation into a political storm that took over ten years to die down, even then failing to leave a satisfactory settlement. Many of his measures were repudiated and he himself was impeached in 1868, escaping dismissal by only the narrowest of margins. Northern Republicans closed ranks and introduced stronger laws to protect blacks, notably the Fourteenth and Fifteenth Amendments of 1866 and 1868, ratified in 1868 and 1870 respectively. Wide powers were taken to lessen Confederate influence in the framing of new state constitutions. For a time Radical Republican state governments were even installed in all the former centers of rebellion. Blacks became active as politicians, judges and even as militiamen, policing the southern states where they had formerly been policed themselves. For a time it looked as though they had achieved something approaching the status they had been led to expect. By the late 1870s, however, all this had turned sour. It was rather the white supremacist, "Johnsonian" version of reconstruction that would hold the field for almost a century thereafter. Many of the laws that remained on Washington statute books failed to trickle down through southern state legislatures to the levels either of local government or of the individual citizen.

Admittedly, Johnson's leniency had to some extent been admirable; it repudiated vengeance and showed suitable magnanimity to the defeated foe as soon as the latter had been disarmed. President Davis, for example, was rounded up by Union cavalry and imprisoned for two years. No charges were ever pressed against him, and he was allowed to take an honorable retirement. Amid the heated passions of the day, such treatment was eloquent of a desire to bury the hatchet as quickly as possible. Among high-ranking Confederates, only the governor of Andersonville prison was hung. His execution was a symbolic condemnation of a multitude of war crimes committed by many men on both sides. The war had lasted far longer than anyone had expected, or wanted, and many Americans had been horrified by the depths of barbarity to which they had found themselves descending. Their relief when the war ended was therefore almost unbounded, and the natural reaction was to try to bury the past. The sealanes were reopened, northern industry continued to boom, and the loss of manpower on the battlefield ended. The North could look forward to a bright future indeed.

The devasted nevertheless found it very hard to return to normality. It was here that Johnson failed to take the decisive lead required in the crucial period immediately following the end of the war. By letting matters drift, Johnson signalled to southern white society that nothing much had been changed by the war, leading the former to increase its demands. Because it had been given this "reward" immediately after Appomattox, society felt confirmed in its old ways and, therefore, doubly resentful of subsequent attempts to change these.

In reality, however, a great deal had been changed both by the war and by simultaneous developments in the international cotton trade. Southern agriculture suffered a body blow from which it could not easily have recovered, even at the best of times. The booming western frontier diverted much-needed capital, energy and skills away from economic reconstruction in the Old South. This made grain America's largest export crop, instead of cotton. New tariffs also raised the prices of manufactured goods imported into the South, which effectively reduced the value of its exports. When the abolition of slavery and the restructuring of traditional elites were added to this, it became clear that a deep social crisis had arrived. Only through a long period of unhappiness and disruption was

any sort of stability to be regained, and even then it was to remain heavily based on the poverty and oppression of black people.

The ex-slaves themselves had at first been delighted with their new freedom, but for many it was not to last. They soon had to confront the harsh realities of making a living under free-enterprise capitalism, often in the very same neighborhoods they had inhabited before. "Black Codes" enacted by state legislatures often tied them down to particular areas, thereby preventing a free market in labor. They had no money to buy land, and too few jobs to go to. Their former masters had neither the capital nor the experience needed to run their farms using hired labor. Wages were depressed and often intermittent. Attempts to solve the problem by sharecropping usually ended in poor returns for the landowner and crippling debts for the freedman. The not dissimilar crop-lien system, introduced by outside money lenders, only made matters worse. In the end many estates had to be sold to northerners, who were widely accused of showing all the vices of traditional southern landowners, but none of their virtues.

New landowners formed only a part of the postwar invasion of the South by carpetbaggers, since they were accompanied by Republican politicians, industrial entrepreneurs, social or religious missionaries, and ex-soldiers. Few of these had sinister motives, and most brought excellently "modern" qualities to the South. Equally the Republican state governments of the first few years displayed many virtues. If they failed, it was partly because the problems they faced were so immense and unprecedented. The major reason for their failure, however, was a lack of continuing support from the North in the face of a conspiracy of resistance from southern whites. Southerners resented the newcomers less for what they did than for what Sherman had done: less for who they were than for what *they* represented. The white South wanted to be left undisturbed by a rapidly changing world, and blamed the messengers of change for the message they brought, rather than themselves for their own inflexibility. They conducted a successful campaign to besmirch the name of the carpetbaggers and their southern scalawag allies. They represented the Republican state governments as hopelessly corrupt, and then destroyed their political base by terrorizing and lynching black voters. By 1876 the Democrats again held control throughout Dixie.

Northern interest in reforming the South had already dissolved in favor of brighter prospects elsewhere. When Grant was elected President in 1868 he represented the moderate Republican desire for reconciliation with the South. He aimed to promote the peaceful expansion of trade and the reduction of government intervention. His administration also was certainly not interested in carrying out interventionist policies in the South. They feared to promote policies that would be hugely expensive and highly damaging to the constitutional rights of the white individual. His administration also became badly tainted by charges of corruption, and lost the moral high ground. By the time of the 1876 presidential elections many northern politicians had also made alliances with southern Democrats, fueling the call for full reconciliation. A cosy agreement was reached, to celebrate the martial glories of the white American soldier, and to forget the political differences of the war together with the civil rights of former slaves.

THE CIVIL WAR
PREWAR

Eli Whitney's saw gin, invented in 1793 and improved by Hogden Holmes in 1796, revolutionized cotton production. Its design allowed the seeds to be removed from American short-staple cotton for the first time. A massive economic boom was the result, and the southern United States led the world in cotton production until about 1941.

A development of the original Whitney gin, this refined and streamlined model made it easier than ever to produce "King Cotton." It was this type of technology that allowed the South to buy and support some 3,200,000 slaves by 1850, disappointing Yankee reformers who had hoped that "The Peculiar Institution" would soon wither away.

SCENE ON A COTTON PLANTATION.   GATHERING COTTON.

The cotton plantation (far left) was undoubtedly both the main drive behind the Southern agricultural revolution, and the main butt of abolitionists. Nevertheless, the vast majority of slaveholders lived outside these highly centralized units of production. Southern frustration was roused by Northern failure to distinguish between the impersonal treatment given to "factory farm" slaves, and the very much softer treatment accorded to the multitude of domestic or "family" ones. Left: black slave in a cotton field. Above: a record load of cotton on a Mississippi steamer. The Mississippi River was as much the South's natural channel for exports to Europe, as it was an entry point to the Midwest. In the War, its loss to the Union would be a major factor in the Confederate defeat.

Far left: shipping cotton from Charleston to foreign, and domestic, parts. In the War, both foreign and domestic outlets would, to a great extent, become blocked, either by Union action or by the inherent inefficiencies of the South's internal distribution network.

Above and left: temperance propaganda from the New England moralists. Most of the world's evils were attributed to alcohol, especially as it was used by the mass of "slovenly" Europeans who came to people the great cities of the North. In some ways these recent immigrants were resented just as much as the Southern slave drivers – and of course they lived much closer to home.

During the first half of the nineteenth century there was a land rush, especially from the Northeast, to the virgin territories west of the Appalachians – to Illinois, Missouri, Kansas, Nebraska, and beyond. Any God-fearing, hard-working person who wanted to start a small farm had only to bring a few oxen, and start to build a log cabin (above). Once the cabin was built (left), the corn would spring up almost on its own, game would be plentiful and the family would flourish. That, at any rate, was the romantic ideal that was widely believed in the North, which wanted the West for its own rapidly expanding population. Note that there was no place in this frontier vision for Southern-style slavery.

THE CIVIL WAR: PREWAR

Emigrants from the North descend the Ohio River in oared houseboats, as part of the general movement to the West in the early nineteenth century.

Fur traders (above) descending the Missouri River, while it was still nearly virgin territory.

U.S. scouts turning back invading "boomers" (left) during the Oklahoma land rush in the unsettled times before the Civil War.

Henry Clay (left), a lawyer and statesman in Kentucky, was the foremost master of constitutional compromises over the status of slaves in the new territories, from the 1820s to his death in 1852. After his death, there would be less talk of compromise. Daniel Webster (above), another Northern statesman of the old school, sought a compromise with the South and the toleration of slavery, but nevertheless championed rapid industrial growth and maximization of Federal power. He died in 1852, at about the same time as many other leading politicians of the same generation, thereby helping open the way for a fresh, less compromising breed. In Abraham Lincoln, this new breed included a key figure who was centrally inspired by Webster's 1830 cry of "Liberty and Union, now and forever, one and inseparable."

Above left: propaganda for the 1856 presidential election, in which the Democrats successfully besmirched the new Republican Party as black-lovers. John C. Fremont – later a prominent, if abysmal, Union general – and his running mate, Dayton, were seen as dangerously abolitionist candidates. They scared off many Southern and conservative supporters.

William Henry Seward (above) was the hard-line anti-compromise, anti-slavery senator from New York who was instrumental in setting up the new Republican Party in 1854. In 1860, he was seen as too radical to win his party's nomination for the presidential election, yet as Lincoln's Secretary of State he would become identified with a much softer view, and would even be reviled as a conservative by abolitionists. From the other side, the Booth gang tried to murder him on the same night Lincoln was assassinated.

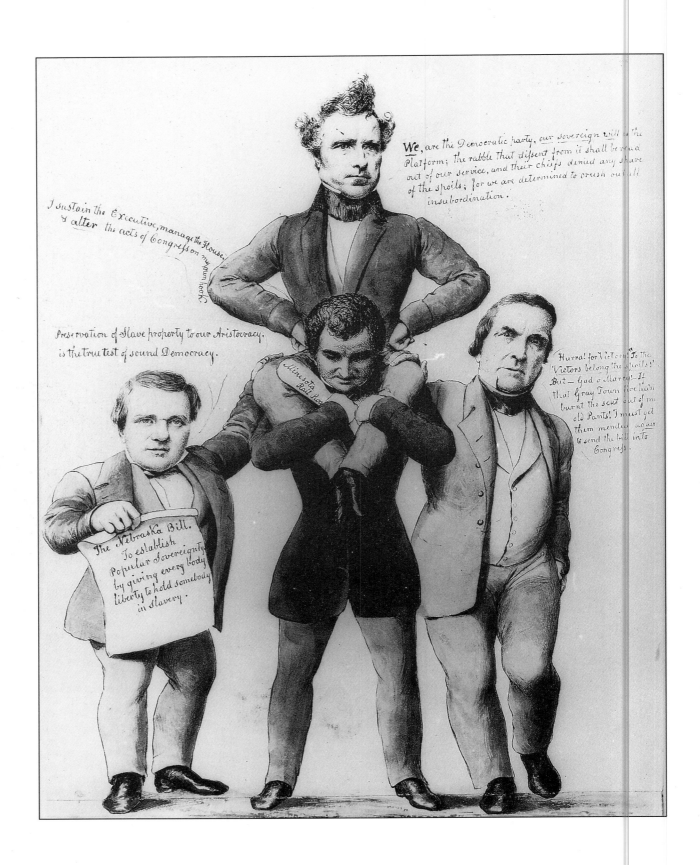

The Kansas debate came to a head with the Kansas-Nebraska bill of 1854, in which the Democrats sided with "squatter sovereignty" as a concealed means of opening the new territories to slavery. In the cartoon (left) the opposition lampoons the bill's champions – Franklin Pierce, sitting on the shoulders of Lynn Boyd, speaker of the house, with Stephen A. Douglas to his right and Thomas Benton to his left. In the event the bill was passed but, unlike in earlier clashes on similar issues, the anti-slavery camp refused to accept the verdict and continued to make fierce challenges that would ultimately tear the nation apart.

Above and above left: Senator Stephen A. Douglas, "the little giant" from Illinois who brilliantly proposed the 1854 Kansas-Nebraska compromise for "squatter sovereignty" in the new territories. His tragedy was that this measure rebounded on him in 1858, when he found that the Southern version of the act, which was also supported by President Buchanan, was unworkable. He then became politically becalmed, was beaten by Lincoln in the presidential election of 1860, and died the following year.

THE CIVIL WAR: PREWAR

Charles Sumner (above), Republican senator for Massachusetts, was one of the outspoken abolitionists who rose to prominence in the 1850s. He helped polarize the two relatively tolerant old-style political parties into bitterly opposed sectional camps for North and South. Later he urged Lincoln to go to war, and when it was over he continued to campaign for civil rights until his death in 1874.

In May 1856 Sumner denounced South Carolina's policies over Kansas from the floor of the Senate. He was set upon and badly beaten (right) by Preston Brooks, a South Carolina congressman. This was one of a series of dramatic incidents that focused popular attention upon the growing political divide. While the North clucked its outrage, the South sent Brooks a sheaf of new sticks.

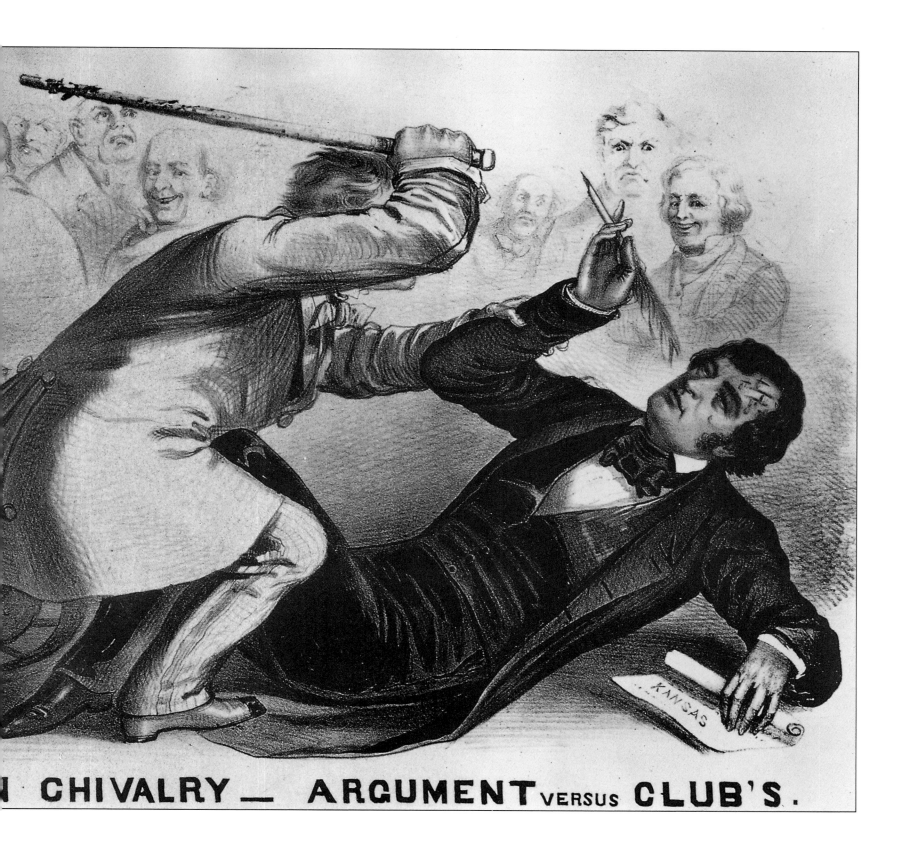

THE DIS-UNITED STATES—A BLACK BUSINESS.

LIBERTY FOR KANSAS.

Far left: Atcheson, Kansas, in the early 1860s. This frontier town had grown quickly from next to nothing, but soon found itself involved in the political battle over whether Kansas should or should not be a slave state. This battle did as much as anything to cause the Civil War. Left: a cartoon demanding liberty for Kansas to decide its own right to keep slaves through "squatter democracy," rather than depending on the diktats of an anti-slavery Federal Government. In the end the Federal Goverment won for the citizens of Kansas the liberty to work as freemen in a free market economy. The *Punch* cartoon (above) could perhaps be accused of making bad puns and hideous stereotypes out of all three of its characters – and of blaming the victim for the crime – but there is some truth in its pictorial placing of the South in the "West" and the North in the "East." However, whereas the North was eventually able to win over much of the West with the promise of land grants, the South, because of its naval inferiority, was unable to expand its initial footholds on the East Coast.

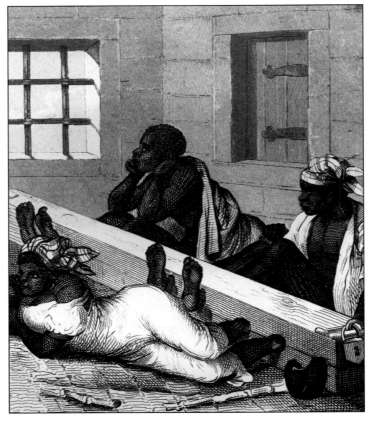

William Lloyd Garrison (above) was the leading 1830s campaigner for the complete abolition of slavery, before that cause had become respectable. In his little journal *The Liberator* and, in his 1832 *Thoughts on African Colonization,* he insisted "I will be heard" – and before very long, he was.

Above, above far left and far left: the anti-slavery lobby's picture of slave misery in Brazil, around 1850. Brazil was often cited as having the most barbarous form of slavery, but the aim of this was more to disgust Americans with their own form than seriously to persuade them to mount an abolitionist crusade to Sao Paulo or Rio de Janiero. Thus did Northern indignation, inspired by the Brazilians, eventually come to be vented on the Confederates.

Above: *Ride for Liberty – The Fugitive Slaves,* Eastman Johnson's celebrated painting of the "underground railroad" by which fugitive slaves were given the hope of freedom, if they could find their way to the North. Legally the 1850 Clay compromise banned such shelter, but in this matter the law was often very hard to enforce in the anti-slavery North. Leon Coffin's Indiana farm (right) was a notable staging point on "the underground railroad" for runaway slaves, as pictured in a famous canvas by Charles T. Webber.

45

Right: John Brown about 1850, at the age of about fifty. Brown was a dedicated activist against all slavery and slavers. He came from a Connecticut family of sixteen children, a total he would himself exceed by fathering twenty of his own. In 1855 he moved to Kansas, where he became the "godfather" of a murderous band of abolitionist terrorists. He was in touch with New England philanthropists, and started to hatch his great scheme for inciting a general slave rising in Virginia. Above: watercolor impression of the "martyrdom" of John Brown, hanged in punishment for leading the 1859 Harper's Ferry raid in which seventeen people died. The aim of the raid was to seize arms from the armory, then set up a guerrilla base in the Virginia hills as the focus for a mass slave rising throughout the South. This strategy is very familiar to modern students of guerrilla warfare, and it can sometimes be very effective. In 1859, however, Colonel Robert E. Lee was able to nip it in the bud with a decisive act of counter-terrorism. The Harper's Ferry armory (far right) in 1864, after it had been raided twice more – by Thomas J. "Stonewall" Jackson, who was on a very different side from John Brown. The armory was then being used as a supply depot for Union troops, who were presumably accustomed to singing the Battle Hymn of the Republic.

Left: Dred Scott, the Missouri slave who claimed his freedom because his master had taken him to live for four years in the non-slave Illinois State and Wisconsin Territory. The Southern-dominated Supreme Court eventually ruled against him early in 1857, in a notorious judgment that seemed to overturn the Missouri Compromise of 1820. Ironically, he was released very soon afterwards by the death of his master, but unfortunately died himself the following year. The Old Courthouse (right) in St Louis, Missouri, was where the Dred Scott case was heard on appeal, in one of its four controversial stages.

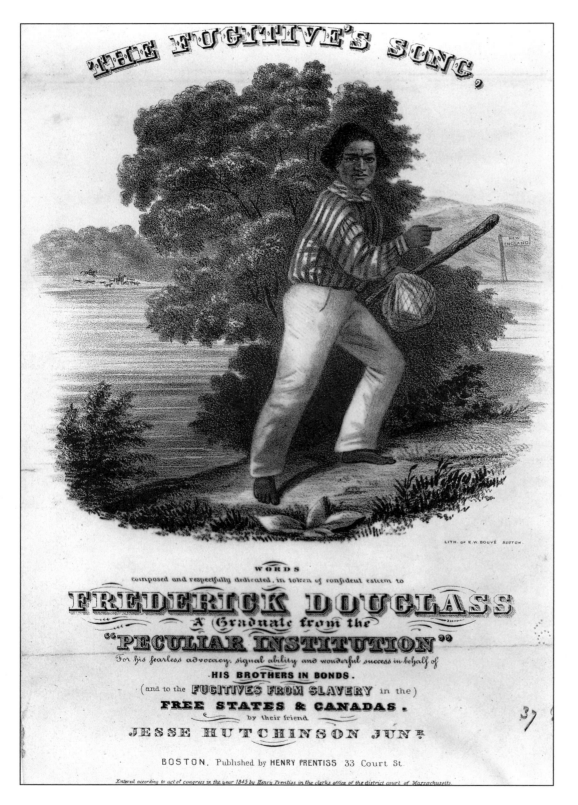

Left: flyleaf of a song composed in honor of Frederick Douglass, the leader of free blacks in the North during the War. Douglass was also a stern critic of Lincoln's belief that whites were a superior race.

Right: Frederick Douglass in old age. He died in 1895, aged seventy-eight.

THE CIVIL WAR
START OF WAR

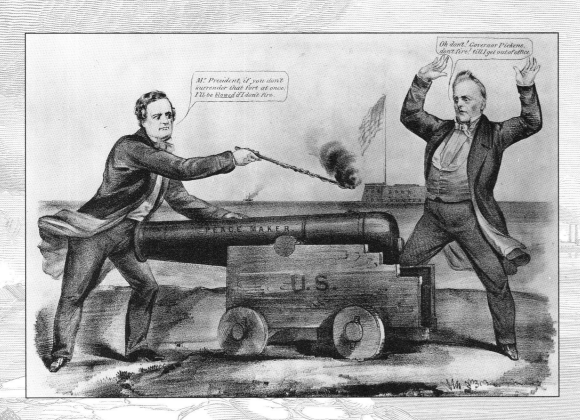

Far left: an excited states' rights demonstration in Savannah, Georgia, during the election campaign of November 1860. The full depth of the South's resentment of Lincoln and the Republicans was understood only dimly in the North at this time, as he did not even run in many parts of the South. His election would be the signal for the first secessions.

Below left: a portrait of the fifteenth President, James Buchanan. A Democrat from Pennsylvania, Buchanan had been seen as capable of placating the South without alienating the North. In the event, however, this put him in a dilemma from which his only escape seemed to be inactivity. During his last few "lame duck" months in office, when secession was breaking out on all sides, he failed to give a clear direction to Federal policy. To this day it remains an open question whether this was due to the constitutional weakness of any president once his successor has been elected, or whether it was because the problem itself was so intractable that only a Lincoln could master it. At any rate it is clear that a Northerner sympathetic to the South certainly could not. A Northern cartoon (left) criticizes Buchanan's failure to extirpate the supposedly suicidal secession threat by Governor Pickens of South Carolina. What the cartoonist misses, however, is both the powerful unity and determination of the Southern people, and the very slender nature of the resources available to coerce them.

THE CIVIL WAR: START OF WAR

Left: Lincoln's first inaugural address, delivered from the steps of the unfinished Capitol on March 4, 1861. Having wrestled for weeks with the agonizing problem of secession, he had still not fully decided on the correct course, and wished to keep as many options as possible open. He therefore expounded his belief that slavery must spread no further, and that secession was wrong but, just as his predecessor had, he remained ambiguous on whether force should be used to restore the Union. Right: a portrait of President Lincoln, who stood for much that the South hated, but not everything that the radical Republican Abolitionists wanted.

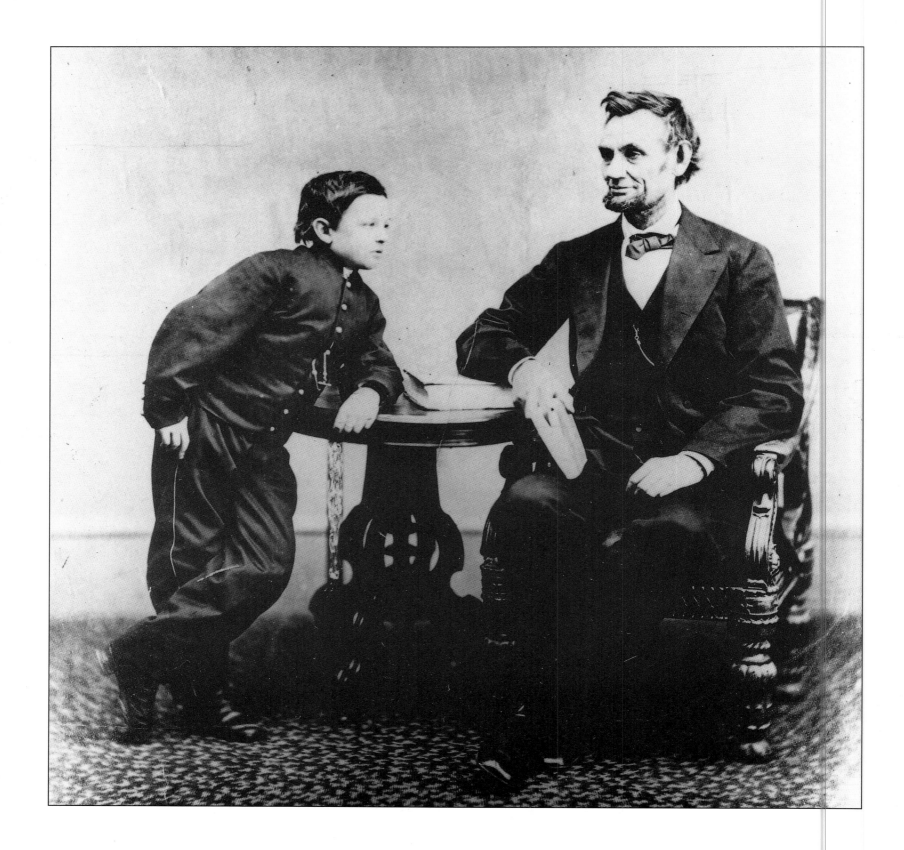

Left: a portrait of President Lincoln with his son, Tad.

Jefferson Davis (right) was the Confederacy's choice as its president. Davis was a man possessing a longer familiarity with both government and war than Lincoln. He had been educated at West Point, fought in Mexico in the 1840s, and held ministerial office in the 1850s. Like Lincoln, he was seen as something of a moderate in the terms of his own section but, unlike his Northern opponent, he lacked the modern party political machinery that might have brought greater efficiency to all the government's operations.

Left: the inauguration of Jefferson Davis in Montgomery, Alabama, on February 18, 1861. The members of his Confederate Government (right) are here rather misleadingly referred to as "chieftains," although they were all civilians!

Left: Major Robert Anderson, veteran of the Seminole wars, who was in command of Fort Sumter when South Carolina seceded from the Union and summoned the fort to surrender. Anderson refused, with the backing of two successive presidents, but was forced to give up after the thirty-four hours' shelling, on April 12-13, 1861, that marked the start of the Civil War. Anderson was later promoted to general, and in April 1865 he would return to Sumter to witness the re-raising of the original flag. Right: the side of Fort Sumter that faced Charleston and the heaviest bombardment.

Interior View of. **FORT SUMTER** on the 14th April 18
after its evacuation by Maj. Robert Anderson, 1st Art: U.S.A. C
Showing the north end of West Barracks, with the two tiers of Casements
Barbette of adjacent north channel face.

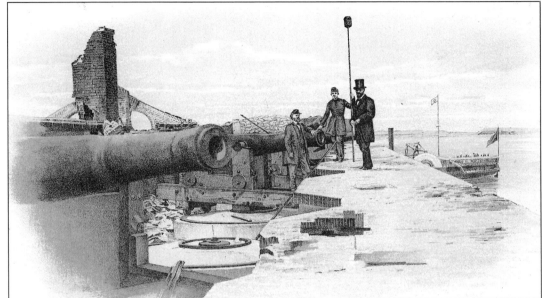

Left: the interior of Fort Sumter after the bombardment and capitulation. Considerable damage has been inflicted and the first Confederate flag – the stars and bars – now flies triumphantly overhead. Strangely, however, no Union soldier was killed during the actual firing. Only one unfortunate artilleryman lost his life, and that was by accident while the fifty-gun surrender salute to the U.S. flag was being fired. Above: the eastern parapet of Fort Sumter after the bombardment, showing some of the damage, together with a sand-bagged barricade against enfilading fire. Obviously Major Anderson had been energetic in preparing for the attack.

Fort Pickens (above) at Pensacola Harbor, Florida, was a federal garrison in the same situation as Fort Sumter. When Florida seceded from the Union, she wanted to take over all Federal property on her soil, but Fort Pickens refused to surrender. Unlike Fort Sumter, however, Pickens was never effectively attacked, and so never fell. It continued to hold out throughout the war, and served as a useful base for later Union operations. At Pensacola itself the Confederates gathered in a camp in Warrington Navy Yard (left). Note the lack of military uniform apart from belts, and the characteristic sunshades constructed out of branches. At least these troops are lucky enough to have proper tents – something that would rapidly become a luxury in the South.

TO THE CITIZENS OF RICHMOND!

The President and the Governor of Virginia, deeply impressed with the necessity of a speedy organization of all able bodied and patriotic citizens, for local defence, in and around the City of Richmond, and throughout the State, urgently appeal to their fellow-citizens, to come forth in their militia organizations, and to commence and perfect at once, other organizations by companies, battallions and regiments. An imperious necessity for instant action exists, and they trust that this appeal will be all that is necessary to accomplish the result. No time is to be lost; danger threatens the City.

Therefore, with a view to secure the individual attention of all classes of the citizens of Richmond, and to impress upon them the full importance of the crisis, it is hereby ordered that all stores and places of business in this City, be closed to-day at three o'clock P. M., and daily thereafter, until further order, and the people be invited to meet and form organizations for local defence. They will be armed and equipped as fast as the companies are formed.

By command of Secretary of War,
S. COOPER,
Adjutant and Inspector General.
By order of the Governor of Virginia,
JOHN G. MOSBY, Jr.,
A. A. A. General.

Left: local recruiting poster for Richmond, Virginia, issued by the state authorities at the start of the War. It took a considerable time for the many local "companies, battalions and regiments" to evolve into standardized organizations in which each could play a coherent part in a unified Confederate army. Meanwhile, each state pursued its own policies for recruitment, supply and even strategy, particularly Virginia herself – a rich and proudly independent state which suddenly found herself fighting in the front line. At least the forces raised via the poster were to be provided with arms and equipment, which was more than could be said for many of the other troops recruited at this time.

Right: the Capitol in Richmond, where the Confederate legislature sat from July 1861. While it was politically prudent to seat its government in one of the more moderate secession states, the Confederacy soon found that Richmond's proximity and tempting accessibility to the North brought heavy fighting to its very gates.

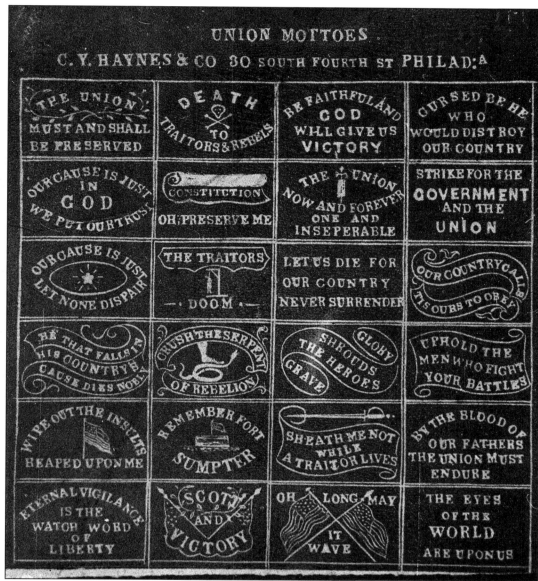

UNION MOTTOES.
C. Y. HAYNES & CO 30 SOUTH FOURTH ST PHILAD:A

One of the early locally raised Confederate companies was the Independent Blues, who were later incorporated into the 3rd Florida Infantry under the more prosaic title of "Company B." Left: their unsubmissive flag. Every bit as unsubmissive is the collection of patriotic Union mottoes (above).

THE CIVIL WAR: START OF WAR

One of the first armed clashes of the war occurred when the 6th Massachusetts Infantry was attacked by a secessionist mob (above) as the regiment marched through Baltimore. This attack outraged Northern opinion, because it seemed to be an act of treachery behind friendly lines. Nevertheless, Maryland was technically a Southern state, and it was rather Washington, D.C., the capital of the Union, that was embarrassingly isolated within the enemy camp.

Left: a more acceptable Philadelphian vision of how troops marching to the front should be received. There is water, coffee, a dining saloon, washing facilities for both men and clothes, and above all a friendly reception from the citizens who are clearly proud of their visiting "sons of North." Ironically, however, the rail line that carries them goes not only to Philadelphia, but also to Baltimore.

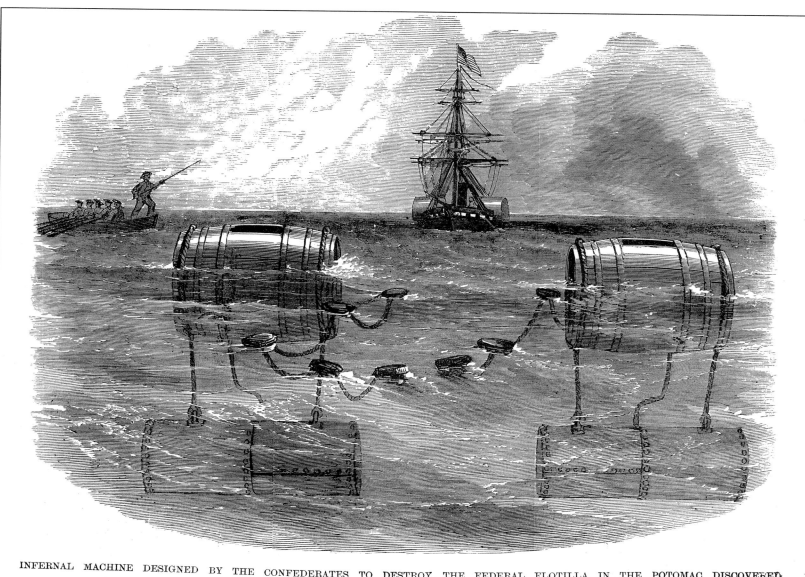

INFERNAL MACHINE DESIGNED BY THE CONFEDERATES TO DESTROY THE FEDERAL FLOTILLA IN THE POTOMAC DISCOVERED BY CAPTAIN BUDD OF THE STEAMER " RESOLUTE."

An "infernal machine" (above) let loose by the Confederates from Aquia Creek into the Potomac River on July 7, 1861. Designed to sink Union warships, it provided a foretaste of the many mines and torpedoes that would be encountered in naval operations throughout the rest of the War.

THE CIVIL WAR: START OF WAR

The Confederate plan for the Battle of First Manassas, or "First Bull Run," was devised by General Pierre G. T. Beauregard (far left), although he was no longer the commander on the day. He had been a keen student of war since his time at West Point, and had lately become the captor of Fort Sumter. He would continue to give excellent service to the Confederacy as one of its most senior generals.

Left: Thomas J. "Stonewall" Jackson, the hero of First Manassas. His brigade held back the Union troops "like a stone wall" until all the latters' enthusiasm for the fight had evaporated. From then until his death at Chancellorsville, he would dazzle the world with his rapid maneuvers and deadly surprise attacks. Many of them have become classics of the military art, just as the men he trained have won lasting glory as his "foot cavalry."

Above: the stone house on the First Manassas battlefield. Situated at the bottom of the slight hill where the main firefight took place, it served as an aid post close behind the Union line – although when that line broke it was soon overrun by Confederates.

The rout of the green Union troops at First Manassas/Bull Run, as represented in a lithograph (above) was an almost accidental event that determined the balance of morale between the two sides in Virginia for at least two years. This battle burst the bubble of Northern confidence, and persuaded the young Army of the Potomac that it was facing near-superhuman opponents. Conversely, it persuaded the Confederates that they had the measure of their enemy, and despite their equal inexperience in warfare, they became convinced they could improve faster, as events indeed proved.

THE CIVIL WAR: START OF WAR

The Union witch hunt after First Manassas/Bull Run was as fearsome as it was irrational. In the drawing (right) by Arthur Lumley, Colonel James E. Kerrigan of the 25th New York Volunteers, who is seated in front of the fireplace, is being charged on nine counts, including drunkenness, and fraternising with the enemy. Such vindictiveness helped make the high command feel better about its defeat, and distracted others from its failings.

Above: the scene in Congress in December, 1861. The winter of 1861-2 was a time of intense political and strategic debate in Washington, D.C., as proponents of the slow but careful "Anaconda Plan" blockading strategy argued against those less patient advisers who had already forgotten Bull Run.

An actual sketch, made on the spot by one the Special Artists of Frank Leslie's Illustrated Newspaper.
Mr. Leslie holds the copyright and reserves the exclusive right of publication.

In the West, 1861 was a vital year for defining the battle lines and winning over wavering allies. Neutral Kentucky and divided Missouri were largely won by the North, although many of their sons would fight for the Confederacy. West Virginia was split from its parent state, as first George McClellan and then John Fremont made over-inflated but fragile reputations out of miniscule campaigns. As an illustration of this, Fremont (far left) is shown "hoisting the American flag on the highest peak of the Rocky Mountains" – a piece of geographical hyperbole out by some two thousand miles.

This page: unknown Confederate soldiers early in the War. The one with braided epaulettes (above center) is a military cadet.

Above: three members of the 3rd Georgia Infantry. Two of them were half brothers, both killed at the battle of Malvern Hill.

Private George W. Livesay (left), of the Virginia Horse Artillery, was killed at Petersburg in 1864. Above: Private Charles Pace of the "Danville Blue" company, 18th Virginia Infantry. Right: Private Walter Miles Parker, who seems to have enlisted with his own shotgun.

Left: Captain George Hillyer, who raised his own company, the Hillyer Rifles, for the 9th Georgia Infantry. Georgia Private Edwin E. Jennison (above), pictured in his best uniform, was killed at Malvern Hill.

THE CIVIL WAR 1862

With the advent of 1862 there was much increased activity in every theater. In the West, General Halleck sat down to the serious task of securing the great rivers, while around the coastline the navy began to make Lincoln's "paper blockade" a reality. A sketch by the famous war artist A. R. Waud shows one of several amphibious expeditions leaving the Chesapeake to seize a fort, or an island, or some other strategic point on the Confederate coast.

A cutout of a Mississippi steamboat – the mainstay of the Western River War.

THE CIVIL WAR: 1862

In the Eastern theater, both sides had dug extensive fieldworks. These arose less as the result of improved firearms, which had been received at this time by only relatively few of the troops, than out of the engineering spirit common among West Point graduates. Something of the scale of the excavations may be glimpsed from the picture of lines at Manassas (above) built by Beauregard over the winter of 1861-2. When the Confederates abandoned the Manassas lines, they left dummies and false cannons made of tree trunks (right) – instantly dubbed "Quaker guns" – so the Union army would believe the lines were still manned.

General George B. McClellan, pictured with his staff (above), was the North's great hope for the spring 1862 campaign to capture Richmond via the Yorktown Peninsula. In many ways McClellan was the most intellectual Northern general, apart perhaps from "Old Brains" Halleck. McClellan had studied the European armies and the Crimean War; he had also designed bayonet training drills and cavalry saddles. In addition, he was a good strategist, who knew how important it was to train his army thoroughly. His fatal defect, however, was that he seemed to lack moral courage when the enemy was nearby. He overestimated their numbers and underestimated the chances of success that an attack might bring. Like a number of his successors who were also educated at West Point, he liked to dig in when he should have been advancing, and to retreat when he should have been standing firm.

The defence of Richmond in the spring of 1862 was first entrusted to Joseph E. Johnston, who failed to break through the Union encirclement at the battle of Seven Pines, or Fair Oaks, on May 31. Johnston was wounded and replaced by Robert E. Lee, who was soon joined on the Chickahominy by Stonewall Jackson, the latter fresh from his triumphs in the Shenandoah Valley. The painting (left) shows, from left to right, Jackson, Johnston and Lee. Lee (right) was the paragon of Southern military heroes. At the start of the War he already had an enviable military record, gained in Mexico and on various internal security campaigns, and both sides were anxious to secure his services. Although no lover of slavery, he eventually opted for service with his home state of Virginia, wherever that might lead. In fact it led to three years in command of the Army of Northern Virginia, and immortality in the annals of history. He was first nicknamed "the ace of spades" for his intensive digging of fortifications around the Confederate capital. However, once his facility in mobile operations had been recognized, he became affectionately known as "Massa Bob."

THE CIVIL WAR: 1862

Before the Peninsular Campaign could start on land, there had been an epic duel of ironclads at sea – the first of its kind in history, and one which has imprinted itself on the imagination of generations. The battle happened because Confederate engineers had been able to improvise a novel armored warship from the wreck of an abandoned Union frigate, the *Merrimac*. The *Merrimac* was a great surprise when it first emerged from its yard in Norfolk, Virginia, to challenge the enemy fleet and sink the wooden warship, the *Cumberland* (above left). However, the *Merrimac* was in turn surprised by the appearance of the Union's experimental *Monitor*. There was a long fight (left) on March 9, before the Confederate vessel eventually succumbed. Above right: John Ericsson, the *Monitor*'s designer, in his glory. Right: the crew of the *Monitor*, grouped around the revolving gun turret that gave it an advantage over the *Merrimac*'s fixed broadsides.

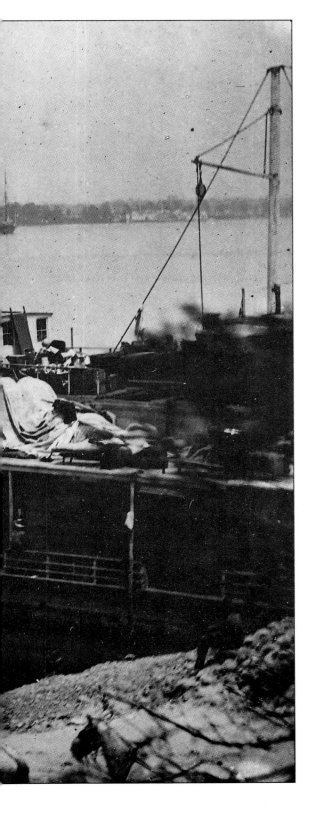

Once the *Monitor* had secured command of the seas around the Yorktown peninsula, the key job of building up supplies for the land army could go ahead, as shown in the photograph (left) taken at City Point, Virginia.

Above: one of the more junior members of the U.S. navy.

While Lee was preparing to renew the attack, General J. E. B. Stuart (left) was busy winning his own immortality, and demoralizing the Union soldiers still further, by mounting a large-scale cavalry raid around the rear of the Union army. Stuart achieved a cavalry supremacy over his opponents that lasted until his death in May 1864 – "the year of exhaustion," when all but the U.S. cavalry had been overextended.

McClellan's army was cut in two outside Richmond by the difficult terrain on either side of the Chickahominy River. He had built a few bridges (below) over this, but large formations coul only file across slowly. This allowed the Confederates to attack sections of the line in turn, without being immediately crushed..

In Lee's "Seven Days' Battle," the Confederates launched several attacks, which usually failed tactically although they did succeed in demoralizing McClellan. One attack that did break through was at Gaines Hill, after which the Union forces tried to cover their retreat by a cavalry charge (right). This was repulsed quickly, with heavy losses.

THE CIVIL WAR: 1862

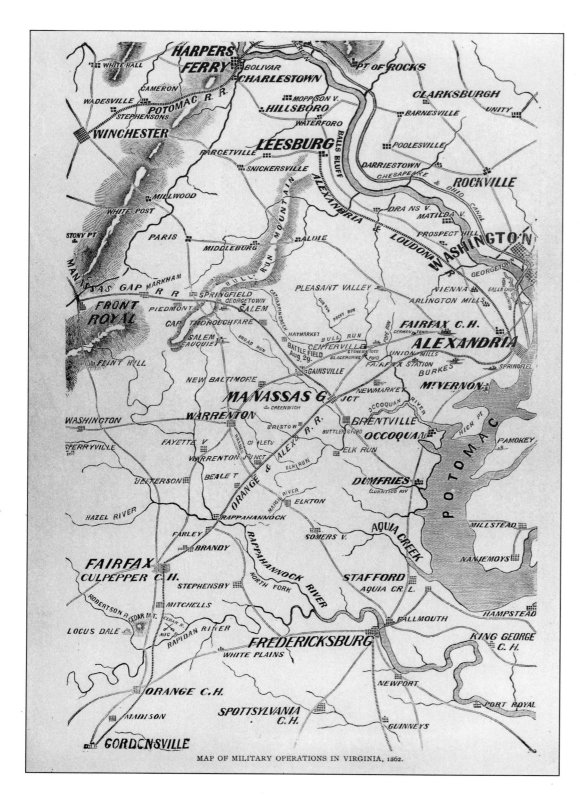

MAP OF MILITARY OPERATIONS IN VIRGINIA, 1862.

The final action of the "Seven Days' Battle" came at Malvern Hill (right) on July 1, when massed Union artillery wreaked havoc on yet another Confederate assault. It was a total victory for McClellan, who still had a great numerical superiority, but who saw this only as evidence that the Confederates must know something he didn't, if they could attack with such futile impetuosity – so he sailed his army back to the Potomac River.

After McClellan's repulse in the Peninsula, another "Western hero" arrived to try his luck in Virginia. This was General John Pope (above), who many alleged was much longer on florid rhetoric than on military common sense. At least he had the excuse that his army was completely green, and that he was facing the notorious combination of Lee and Jackson at their prime. However that may be, he was severely beaten at the Second Manassas/Bull Run on August 29-30. Left: a map of northeast Virginia, scene of many 1862 campaigns.

Left: fugitive blacks fording the Rappahannock River to escape Jackson's unexpected advance in August 1862.

After Second Manassas, Lee determined to advance into Union territory at last, both to bring the war to the enemy and to win some European allies. There was much goodwill towards the Confederacy in Europe but, as the cartoon (right) points out, Uncle Sam somehow always seemed a bit too big. Davis and Lee hoped that the capture of Washington would make him look a little smaller.

Above right: Jackson's "foot cavalry" wading the Potomac River at White's Ford. They are shown taking off their boots and pants but, after the hard campaigning, many of them would have had all too little of either to take off. Shoe leather especially was always at a premium in the underequipped Army of Northern Virginia.

"RECOGNITION," or "NO."

J. BULL *to* NAPOLEON III. "Can you recognize that thing they call the C. S. A.?"
NAP. "Well, I think I could, if 'twere not for that Big Fellow who stands in front."

THE CIVIL WAR: 1862

Lee was brought to battle along Antietam Creek, near Sharpsburg, on September 17. It was a fiercely fought day - "America's bloodiest" - with Union attacks and Confederate counterattacks being repeatedly repulsed until neither side could carry on. General Burnside's Union troops (above) make heavy going across the creek over what is now known as the "Burnside Bridge." Note that in reality the hill defended by the Confederates was steeper and higher than depicted here.

Right: engraved map of the Antietam battlefield area. The Confederates held Sharpsburg and the line of the creek facing East, but their position was vulnerable because of the Potomac River to their rear.

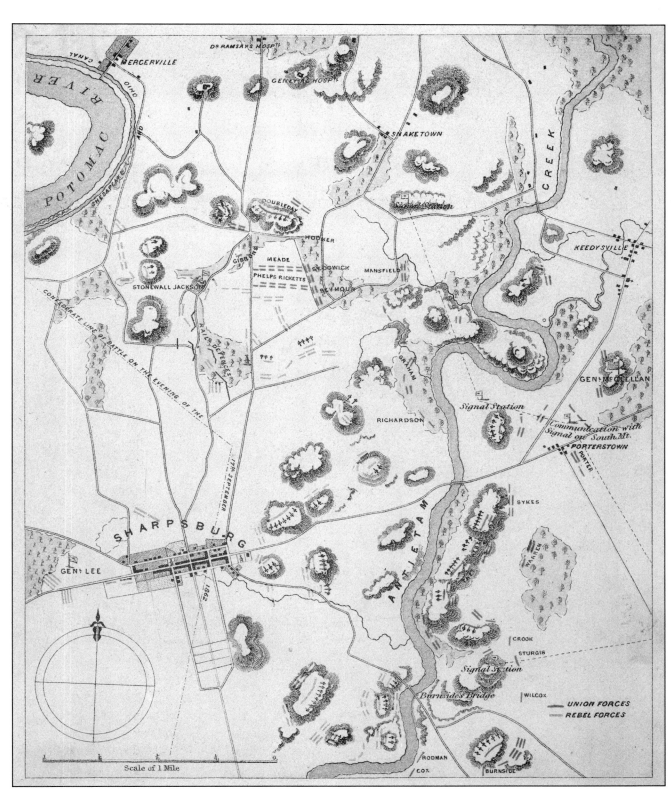

A famous image of the carnage at Antietam (left), when the North lost 2,108 men, and the South 2,700. Total casualties were around 10,000 and 12,000 respectively, which constituted approximately one fourth of all the troops actually committed to combat. This number is high, but it is by no means exceptional, or even shocking, by the standards of European warfare in the nineteenth and twentieth centuries.

After Antietam Lincoln issued his Emancipation Proclamation, then came to visit the battlefield. He is seen (right) with McClellan, at right, and his intelligence chief, Major Allan Pinkerton of the famous detective agency, at left. Some of McClellan's habitual caution may be attributable to the inflated reports submitted by the latter officer, but Lincoln was in no mood to make the distinction. He replaced McClellan with Burnside a month after this photograph was taken.

The North never wished to give either equality or even racial respect to blacks, but only to give them liberty from the specific institution of slavery, and that only in the northern and western territory at first. The more general Emancipation Proclamation of September 22, 1862, was thus extracted from a rather reluctant and diffident President Lincoln. It seems he shared the widespread belief that blacks were inferior, and fit only for menial tasks with low wages. It was certainly in this capacity that the Union employed several hundred thousands of them, such as the dock workers (left). The most "noble" status to which most blacks could aspire was as a soldier (right and below) in the Northern army. Alas, for many of them the bold martial image was often tarnished by exceptionally bad conditions, even by army standards, and, once again, by menial tasks with low wages.

THE CIVIL WAR: 1862

On only a relatively few occasions did black units fight in the front line, although when they did so they acquitted themselves well. They were also targetted by the Confederates for especially ferocious treatment, as in one 1862 bloodhound attack (left). Below: successful fighting by black troops at Milliken's Bend on the Mississippi River, early in 1863.

General Ambrose E. Burnside (right) was yet another example of a man who had made his name in a minor theater before rising to command the Army of the Potomac. In his case the victory had been not in the West, but on the North Carolina coast. He was a competent corps commander, not to mention the inventor of a patent rifle, among several other achievements, but he himself protested that he would be out of his depth in command of a large army; and so, alas, it proved.

BATTLE OF

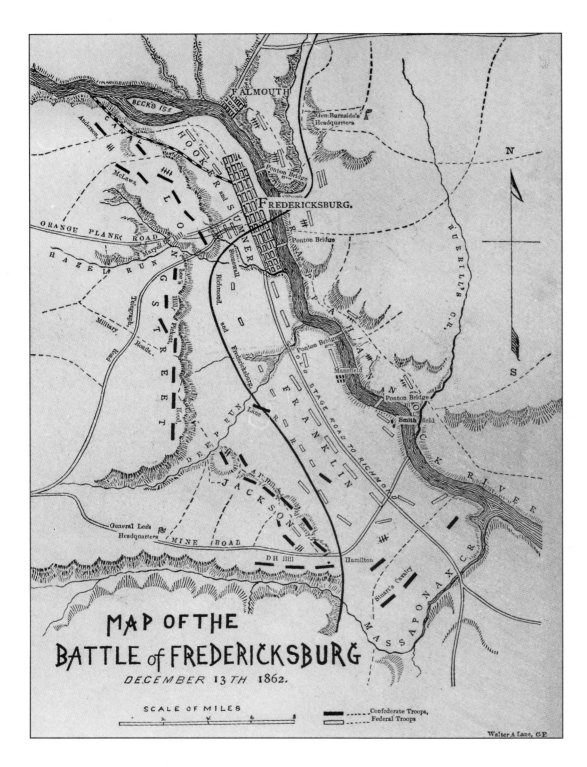

MAP OF THE
BATTLE of FREDERICKSBURG
DECEMBER 13TH 1862.

SCALE OF MILES

Confederate Troops,
Federal Troops

Walter A Lane, C.E.

Left: a map of the Battle of Fredericksburg. By December, Burnside had assembled his army on the left bank of the Rappahannock River, facing Lee's army on the right bank. All he had to do was replace the destroyed bridge (right), cross the river, seize the town and then storm the defended heights that lay beyond. In theory it sounded perfectly possible, especially since the Union enjoyed superiority in artillery as well as in infantry, but in practice it led to something approaching a disaster.

THE CIVIL WAR: 1862

Rebel Pickets death in Fredericksburg.
Ponton Bridge; Union Batteries firing on the rebel works back of the city

Confederate resistance along the river bank at Fredericksburg was not great, consisting merely of the galling fire of sharpshooters, although this did considerably delay bridge building. A sketch (left), probably by the war correspondent Edwin Forbes, depicts Confederate shaprshooters killed by return fire. The massed Union assault on the town of Fredericksburg (right) met relatively little resistance, but the town itself suffered great damage – first from the preparatory artillery bombardment, and then from the unrestrained looting (below left), sketched by Arthur Lumley. That a town still containing civilians could be treated in this way sent a shock wave of horror across the continent and set an evil precedent both for the scorched earth strategies of 1864-5, and on into the twentieth century.

THE CIVIL WAR: 1862

Above: Mathew Brady's historic first photograph of troops in actual combat, under fire at Fredericksburg. Admittedly the fire was probably at very long range, since these guns are doubtless in the main Union gun line east of the river, and the gunners exhibit an unhurried and unworried calm as if still at drill.

The main Confederate defense line just to the west of Fredericksburg was defined by the road and the stone wall at the foot of Marye's Heights. Dead defenders (right) lay behind the line after it had been captured in the battle of May 1863, but on December 13, 1862, it was still an impregnable fortress. The carnage shown here within the position must have been as nothing to the more than 6,000 Union casualties suffered on the other side of the wall in the earlier battle. The dead and wounded were then spread like a carpet across an open field – most of them between 100 and 300 yards from the wall. After that, Burnside had to give up the attempt to capture Fredericksburg.

A few days after Fredericksburg, between December 31 and January 2, Confederate General Braxton Bragg (far left) met Union General William S. Rosecrans (left) at Murfreesboro on Stone's River, Tennessee. Like Lee at Antietam, Bragg was raiding to the north but had been run to ground by superior forces. His army fought magnificently, but eventually it had to retire. The Battle of Murfreesboro (below left) was fought on terrain more thickly encumbered with cedar trees than that shown, making orderly formations a tactical impossibility. The toll of casualties was no less high than in the many other "slaughter pens" of 1862, amounting to some 11,000 Confederate and 13,000 Union losses.

Left: repairing a broken railroad after the Battle of Murfreesboro. As the war progressed, the North greatly expanded its ability to lay and repair rails, whereas Southern industry could not keep up with all the many demands made upon it. The railroads of Dixie became ever more unreliable and intermittent in their services, while those of the North became ever more efficient.

Above: as 1862 drew to a close, it was still possible to believe that God would indeed "Save the South." Although Lee's Army of Northern Virginia had not yet won the War, it had certainly thrashed the Army of the Potomac on almost every occasion they had met. In the West there had been failures, but these had not yet been decisive enough to prove that victory had slipped out of reach. Right: the opposite view was pithily expressed in a Northern cartoon.

THE CIVIL WAR 1863

Above: A. R. Waud's sketch of Burnside's ignominious "Mud March" in late January 1863. The idea was to outflank the Fredericksburg position that had proved impenetrable in December, but the movement simply became bogged down in wind, rain and bottomless roads. As they crawled laboriously past enemy lines, the mood of the Yankee soldiers was scarcely lightened by large panels set up by the Confederates that summed everything up in the words "Burnside Stuck In The Mud."

After his "Mud March" Burnside was replaced as commander of the Army of the Potomac by the brash General Joseph "Fighting Joe" Hooker (above), who immediately set about making many necessary reforms in the cavalry and staffwork and in the building of morale. He then repeated Burnside's outflanking plan, resulting in the Battle of Chancellorsville between April 27 and May 4, 1863. To some Americans, however, Joe Hooker's name will be more familiar for the way it entered the language following the activities of some of his troops while they were quartered in Washington, D.C.

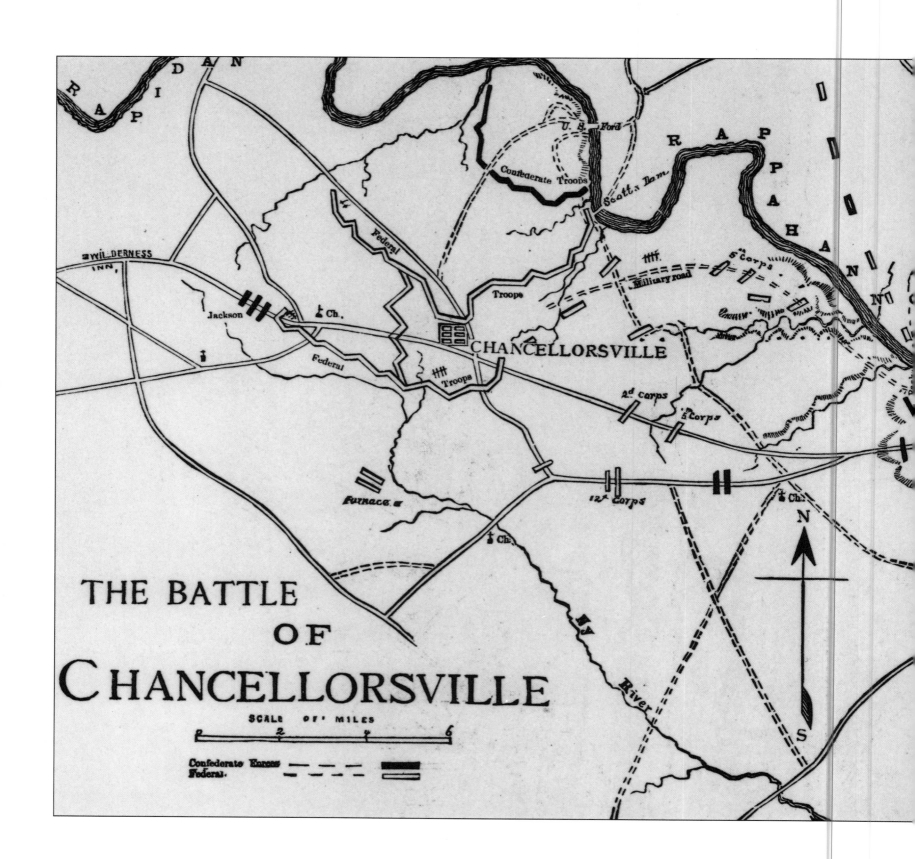

ROBERT EDMUND LEE.
COMMANDER-IN-CHIEF OF THE CONFEDERATE FORCES.

Far left: map of the fighting grounds of Fredericksburg and Chancellorsville. Hooker's plan was to march northwest from Fredericksburg, then ford the Rapidan River to Chancellorsville in order to take Lee's army from the rear. Unfortunately for the Union, however, Lee predicted this would happen and launched a series of fierce spoiling attacks before Hooker could shake free from the Wilderness Woods around Chancellorsville. The Union troops fell onto the defensive and, despite their numerical superiority, retreated to their starting positions. Above: Confederate artillery vehicles hit by Union artillery on Marye's Heights, Fredericksburg, towards the end of the Chancellorsville fighting. Chancellorsville was in many ways the most brilliant victory for Lee (left), in which maneuver, bluff and surprise had all played a vital role. It was a victory blighted, however, by the death of Stonewall Jackson after he was accidentally shot by one of his own sentries.

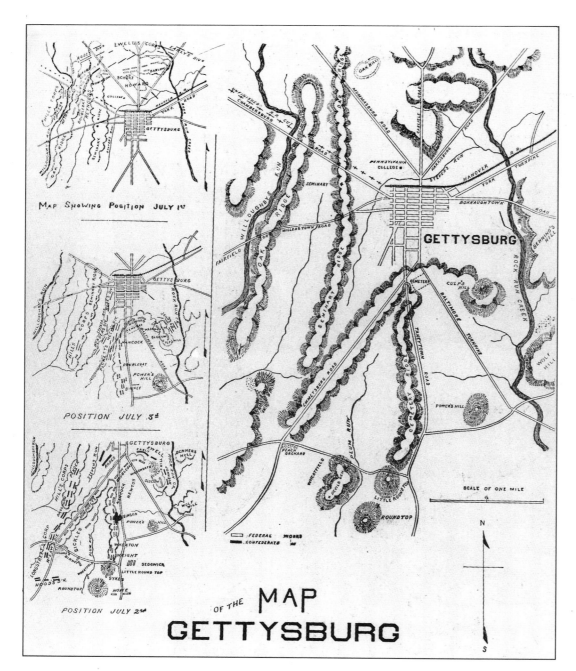

Left: map of Gettysburg, Pennsylvania. After Chancellorsville Lee again felt confident enough to invade the North – a movement which reached its high-water mark at Gettysburg, where the greatest battle of the War was fought between July 1 and 3. Above: the town of Gettysburg from the area of Culp's Hill. Early in the battle, the Confederates fought through into the town, then deployed on either side of it beneath the horseshoe of high ground held by the Army of the Potomac, now commanded by General Meade, who had replaced Hooker after the Chancellorsville failure.

Right: the 1855 gates to Evergreen Cemetery, at the center of the Union position at Gettysburg. The Confederates failed to seize this on the first day, when it was only lightly defended, and were then beaten back from it later, when it had been reinforced. The cemetery itself was dedicated by Lincoln as the Soldiers' National Cemetery on November 19, 1863, the occasion of his celebrated Gettysburg Address.

THE CIVIL WAR: 1863

Above left: the Union guns of Stevens' battery in action near the Gettysburg cemetery, sketched by A. R. Waud. Left: Charles Reed's picture of field artillery being maneuvered on the "prolong" - ropes enabling infantry to drag the gun without the need for vulnerably conspicuous horses. At Gettysburg a high proportion of the casualties were caused by field artillery, especially by the 372 Union pieces that enjoyed the advantage of a defensive posture against waves of attacking infantry. On the second day of the battle, Lee ordered General James Longstreet (above) to attack the Union left flank. If the attack had been launched with speed and energy it might well have seized the two Round Top Hills, the key to the battlefield. In the event, however, the Round Tops were stoutly defended, and only Sickles' overextended 3rd Corps was pushed back to Cemetery Ridge, where it should have been posted in the first place.

Above: Forbes' painting of artillery on Little Round Top. Right: victims of the bitter fighting for the Round Tops and Devil's Den.

The Abraham Trostle Farm (above left), located below the center of Cemetery Ridge, was behind the Union line at the start of July 2, but was captured by the Confederates on that day. Bigelow's 9th Massachusetts Battery was overrun with the loss of four out of six guns, and some fifty horses. Left: more vicitims of the bitter fighting for Devil's Den. Right: fallen soldiers of the 3rd Union Corps near Rose Farm – part of Sickles' overextended line. These bodies were photographed by Alexander Gardner very soon after the battle, but in order to secure a scoop he misnamed them as those men who had fallen at the side of the Union hero General Reynolds on the first day and some two miles further north. Above: panorama of the battle on its third morning, viewed from the rear of the Union lines. Culp's Hill is on the right of the horizon, Cemetery Hill is just left of center, and Cemetery Ridge, against which Pickett's charge would shortly be launched, is beyond the copse to the left of that – where the artist has noted "Union artillery on brow of hill."

THE CIVIL WAR: 1863

Confederates bridging the Shenandoah River (above) in their long retreat from Gettysburg, three weeks after the battle. This was a strategic move that would initiate many months of thrust and parry between the two sides in Virginia without a major battle being fought.

After two years of war, the flow of genuine volunteers for the Union army had dried up, and increasingly desperate measures had to be taken to attract recruits (above right) – notably the use of cash bounties. Unfortunately the big cities such as New York proved to be full of desperate foreigners, down-and-outs and petty criminals, who were only too delighted to accept 677 dollars for a few days' military service before they deserted to take another bounty elsewhere. Big cash bounties were thus not the answer to the army's manpower needs, so both sides were forced to resort to the draft. In the South this had hit all white males equally and early, but in the North it came quite late, and was selective, following the French pattern. Right: a draft lottery in New York. Not only did this practice seem unfair to, and was bitterly resented by, its potential victims, but the army did not like the quality of soldier it produced. This should not have come as any surprise, however, since exactly the same thing had already been noted in France itself.

THE CIVIL WAR: 1863

At the very height of the Gettysburg campaign the patience of New Yorkers ran out, and they mounted a terrible series of riots. Left: an incendiary attack in Lexington Avenue.

Later the mob took on a still uglier mood, and turned its wrath against all blacks. Many were lynched (below), in one of New York City's most discreditable episodes.

Right: a map of the Fortress of Vicksburg.

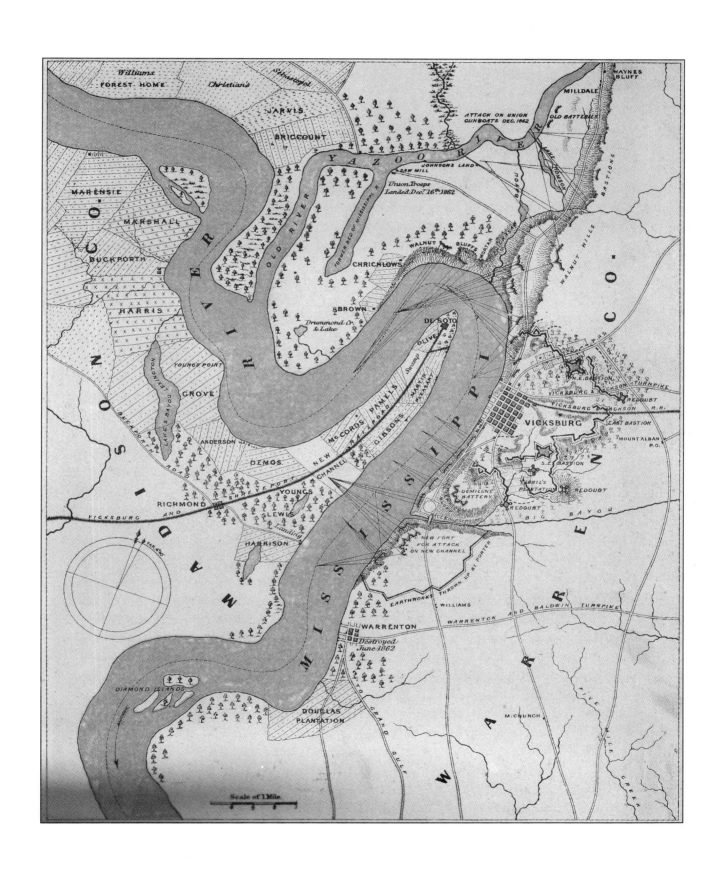

THE CIVIL WAR: 1863

Simultaneously with the Gettysburg campaign, the great siege of Vicksburg was taking place for the control of the Mississippi River. The Union army's problem was to find a practicable approach by water that would enable a complete encirclement of the city. It suffered numerous failures, such as the armored steamship Cairo (left), designed by the self-educated James Buchanan Eads, which attempted to open the Yazoo River in December 1862 only to be sunk by the first ever use of an electrically detonated mine, or torpedo. Below left: lithograph of the steamboats *Baltic* and *Diana* on the Mississippi River.

Eventually, in March 1863, General Ulysses S Grant – one of several rising Western generals whose reputations were built on solid foundations – began an ambitious land march to outflank Vicksburg through the wild territory to the west. This was to be supported by Admiral Porter's flotilla (above right) running down the Mississippi River at night, under the very noses of the Confederate batteries. Several naval encounters (right) were the direct result of this strategy.

After Grant had maneuvered to surround the fortress, a long siege ensued with much desperate fighting, including close-quarter combat (above) with hand grenades.

Right: the Union trenches at Vicksburg seen from behind. Men rest in shelters cut into the hillside, while heavily fortified snipers and gun crews take potshots through loopholes. Unlike in twentieth-century battles, in the Civil War there was little danger from indirect fire, hence the trenches had to be strong to the front and flanks, but did not need overhead protection.

$1,000!
REWARD.
Head Quarters U. S. Forces,
Columbus, O., Nov. 28, 1863.
GEN. JOHN H. MORGAN
Captains J. C. Bennett, L. B. Taylor, L. D. Hockersmith, Sheldon T. H. Haines, and G. S. Magee,
Escaped from the Ohio Penitentiary on the night of the 27th instant.
A Reward of $1,000!
Will be paid for the apprehension and arrest of John Morgan, and a suitable reward for the apprehension and arrest of the others.
WM. WALLACE,
Colonel 15th O. V. I. Commanding.

In April 1862, twenty-two Union soldiers, in disguise, infiltrated south to Big Shanty, near Kenesaw, Georgia. They seized the locomotive, the *General* (left), and drove it hell for leather northward towards Chattanooga, attempting to destroy bridges and block the tracks as they went. They were pursued as far as Ringgold and prevented from completing the planned destruction, which might have had serious strategic implications. Eight of the raiders were hanged, including their leader, James J. Andrews. After this experience both the importance and the vulnerability of the Western railroads were well noted by both sides, and the war entered a new phase. 1863 saw developments in the deep cavalry raids that had been pioneered by Stuart in the East. One of the most spectacular was that by the veteran Confederate railroad wrecker, John H. Morgan. In July he was supposed to take 2,500 cavalry through Kentucky, but on his own authority he kept going into Ohio, almost reaching Pennsylvania. He was arrested, and jailed, but escaped in November (above) to resume his raiding career.

Above: some 1863 model Confederate carbines that Morgan's men might have carried, although many of them would have carried only shotguns, pistols or ordinary infantry weapons. The first three, from the top, are based on the standard Enfield rifle, manufactured respectively by Cook in Athens, Georgia; the Richmond armory; and the Tallassee, Alabama, armory. The weapon at the bottom is a rare Confederate manufactured breechloader, by Jere H. Tarpley of North Carolina.

Right: the area between Murfreesboro and Chickamauga.

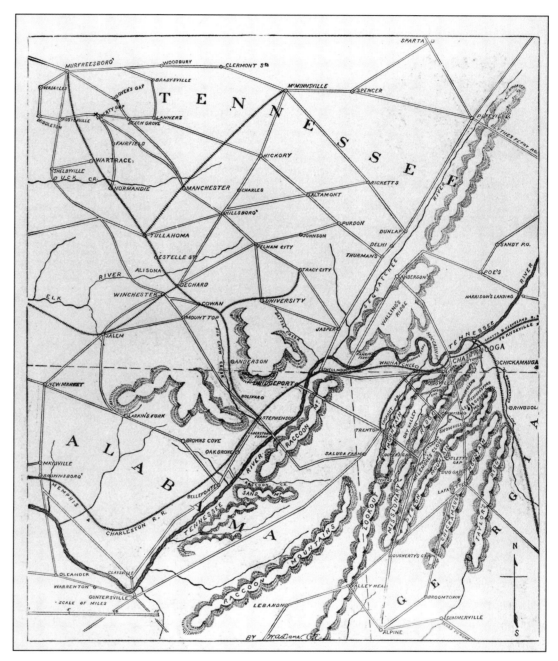

THE CIVIL WAR: 1863

The big Western battle in the fall of 1863 was fought on Chickamauga Creek, where Rosecrans' pursuit of Bragg was brutally reversed by a Confederate counterattack on September 19-20. The woodcut (above) seems to have been imagined from a variety of third-hand accounts of the terrain and breastworks, although the Brotherton cabin, in the center, is just recognizable. The other germ of truth it contains is the idea that General George H. Thomas held out against the otherwise successful Confederate breakthrough.

Left: General John B. Hood, who had led more successful Civil War infantry assaults by this time than practically any other commander. Hood's arm had been withered at Gettysburg while he was fighting at the head of a division, and now, at Chickamauga, he lost a leg.

Right: artist's impression of Hood being wounded at Chickamauga. After Chickamauga, the Confederates imposed an open siege on Chattanooga (below right), only to find that their own supply lines - by rail through Dalton - were more badly strained than those of their opponents, who controlled both the Tennessee River and the state. General Grant came to take command of the defense, and between November 23 and 25 he launched a devastating counterattack that chased Bragg's army away from their lines of investment.

THE CIVIL WAR: 1863

Left: the camp and regimental drill of the 96th Pennsylvania Infantry at Camp Northumberland. The regiment is drawn up in a column of ten companies, each in a two-deep line with a frontage of around twenty men. Very few Civil War soldiers entered hostilities with any previous military experience, although they were certainly anxious to learn. This usually meant that they studied close-order drill for many hours each day, and little else. This gave them the habit of fighting in dense columns that were especially vulnerable to enemy fire. Below: regiment drawn up in column of half companies for marching, in the Arlington training camp. Many of the regiments destined for the Army of the Potomac began their service with an intense drill course at Arlington under the eye of General Silas Casey, who was the author of an influential drill manual.

Large-scale formal field days were often held when troops were in camp, and in winter there were sometimes informal ones (right) based on inter-brigade snowball fights. It was found that the best results were obtained in snowball fighting if each regiment maintained formation around its flag, and maneuvered according to its drills, exactly as it would in a real battle.

Below: drums of the 93rd New York Infantry regiment in Virginia, 1863. The regimental band was an important aid to keeping regular time in combat drill, but fighting formations became less regular as the war continued, so bands often fell out of use. The Union's Western armies were particularly famed for their lack of regularity, and would scornfully refer to their Eastern comrades as "the bandbox Army of the Potomac."

THE CIVIL WAR: 1863

Above: a Sutler's store. When the army stayed in one place for more than a few days, quite elaborate free enterprise trading posts would open. Their attraction was that they could supply the soldiers with little luxuries unobtainable through the official army commissariat.

Noncommissioned officers of Company D, 93rd New York Infantry (left), enjoy a very civilized meal in Virginia, August 1863. Rarely for the time the officers are sitting up to a table and on folding chairs. Note the pile of crackers at the center front of the table. Note also the fact that no less that fifty per cent of those present have removed their hats – a unique occurrence among all the photographs in this book!

Soldiers often built quite elaborate, and warm, log huts (right) for their winter quarters, each of which might be occupied by two to four men, or even a whole squad. In the center of this picture is the squad cook holding his knife and the squad kettle. Note the corduroy path - a necessary antidote to the mud wherever troops settled down during the winter months.

News vendors (left) would often stroll through the camp calling out for customers. All modern studies of combat morale emphasize the importance to the fighting soldier of plentiful news from home. In this respect the Civil War soldier was exceptionally well served by nineteenth-century standards, both in terms of newspapers and in the efficient postal system that kept him in contact with his family and loved ones. Right: a horse-drawn newsstand serving the Union army at Culpeper in 1863.

THE CIVIL WAR
1864

General William T. Sherman was Grant's ablest lieutenant in the Western campaigns, during which they both arrived at the conclusion that pitched battles were generally indecisive, not least because of logistic limitations on the pursuit phase, but also because scorched earth raiding was more effective in making the war bite on the enemy economy, government and people. After the Battle of Chattanooga, therefore, Sherman's policy became to avoid battle, but to devastate the Southern economy.

The Union advance from Chattanooga to
Atlanta encountered a series of very elaborate
lines of fieldworks dug by J. E. Johnston. Sherman
usually confronted them, feinted to one side
and then outflanked to the other, thereby
forcing the Confederates to retreat to their
next line.

In the Western theater, the primary means of transportation for any army was the river steamer. If the army had to operate away from the rivers, however, as Sherman did when he cast loose from Chattanooga and the Tennessee River, it had to use another available system – the railroad. Enormous efforts were made, especially by the Union, to keep the rails open. The new 780-foot trestle bridge (left) is protected by troops and blockhouses. Right and below right: Sherman's men destroying railroads at Atlanta – not only to wreck the Confederate economy, but also to cut off their own line of supply. The aim was to make pursuit impossible, and to feed their own men on the march to the sea using only what they could carry themselves, and what the countryside could be made to yield. To destroy a railroad beyond repair, the technique was to make a bonfire of the ties, bring the rails to white heat over this, then use special hooks to twist them round into an unusable shape that was known as a "Sherman neck tie."

THE CIVIL WAR: 1864

Above: a painting depicting Sherman's soldiers destroying the railroad tracks on their march to the sea.

Below: a family of refugees attempting to escape the horrors of war. The policy of scorched earth created great destitution not only among the agents of the enemy government, but also among the general population.

While Sherman secured his hold on Georgia, the Confederate General Hood lunged north in desperation, attempting to find the "soft underbelly" of the Union army in Tennessee. Despite a brilliantly conceived strategic approach, however, he met a completely new army, under Thomas, at Franklin and then at Nashville. The Battle of Nashville (right) on December 15-16 destroyed the last major Confederate army in the West.

THE CIVIL WAR: 1864

Meanwhile in the Eastern theater General Grant had taken command of the Union armies, and for his 1864 spring campaign, he started to advance on Richmond through the Wilderness and the old Chancellorsville battlefield. This campaign was marked by bloody assaults on Confederate fortifications that were then seldom captured, followed by exhausting outflanking night marches that Lee could usually counter in time. At least the deliberate firing of trees (above) to illuminate the route to be followed seems to indicate that the staff work had improved.

One of the bloodiest assaults in the approach to Richmond was at Cold Harbor (right) on June 3, when the Union suffered 7,000 casualties in half an hour, and then had to face over a week of trench warfare.

Left: excavating human remains at Cold Harbor – in this case doubtless those from the 1862 combats on the same ground, rather than from Grant's recent assault. Soldiers who marched back over this area, on their way home after the War, remarked on the large numbers of fat black crows that it seemed to have attracted. After Cold Harbor, Grant neatly sidestepped Lee to the south – at last – but came up against the formidable defenses of Petersburg. Here the exhausted armies settled down to ten months of trench warfare – often with very far fewer men per yard of frontage than in the hectic massed battles of 1862-3. A. R. Waud's sketch (below left) of the firing line on August 18 shows at least a yard between each man.

In the Petersburg siege there was a marked increase in indirect artillery fire, and hence a greater need than there had been up to this point in the Civil War for overhead cover and bombproof shelters. The 13-inch Dictator (above), mounted on a special railroad flatbed, was one of the heavier mortars deployed by the Union. Right: another heavy railroad gun at Petersburg. Because this one is not a mortar but a direct fire gun, it has been equipped with a shield to protect its crew.

Left: the Union arsenal at City Point, Virginia. This was the central dump for munitions landed from ships to supply Grant's army around Petersburg. On August 11, there was a terrific explosion (right) in Grant's ammunition dump at City Point, near Petersburg. It was claimed to be a Confederate act of sabotage.

THE CIVIL WAR: 1864

While the main armies were becoming involved in the siege of Petersburg, a secondary campaign was being fought in the Shenandoah Valley to the northwest. Here General Jubal A. Early (left), a notable veteran of almost every campaign in the east, was able to open up a wide path ahead of himself. By July 11 he had arrived at the gates of Washington itself, and even, it is said, came under the eyes of President Lincoln. He could advance no further, however, and had to retire regretfully back into Virginia. In the October 19 Battle of Cedar Creek (below) Early was initially successful, but he suffered a devastating counterblow when General Philip H. Sheridan arrived on the scene. Sheridan was in the process of perfecting his hard-hitting new cavalry corps, and was able to show off its splendid combination of mobility and firepower at Cedar Creek. At Appomattox the following year it was destined to be still more devastating.

Right: Lincoln's second inaugural address. Just as Washington, D.C. began to recover from the excitement of Early's invasion, it became centrally involved in a new presidential election. General George McClellan ran for the Democrats, but the national mood heavily backed the sitting Republican president for a second term. Too much blood had been spilled for there to be any compromise, or any weakening of the established authorities that had run the War from its start.

THE CIVIL WAR: 1864

Above: an encounter between a blockade runner and a Union man of war. 1864 was the year in which the Union blockade really began to bite hard. Not only were more Confederate ports and coastal positions falling to direct attack, but naval operations against blockade runners at last went into top gear. From their staging points in the Bahamas the blockade runners had only relatively short distances to travel. They could never be entirely stopped, but at this period their risk of capture rose dramatically.

When the Confederates tried to regain occupied parts of their coastline they sometimes met with success, as in the counterattack on Plymouth, North Carolina, in April. This was led by the heavy ironclad ram *Albemarle* (below left). However, a daring small boat raid by USN lieutenant, William B. Cushing, succeeded in sinking her in October by exploding a torpedo against her side. Left: a Confederate torpedo boat, typical of the cheap new technology that was rapidly changing the face of the Civil War at sea.

THE CIVIL WAR: 1864

In December 1864, a Union attempt to capture Fort Fisher – the key to Wilmington, North Carolina – ended in fiasco. It was commanded by General Benjamin F. Butler, one of the last of the early-war political appointments, and a man who rarely showed signs of true military competence. He was promptly replaced by General Alfred H. Terry, and a new assault (above) in January was finally successful. Right: the interior of Fort Fisher under attack. The fort was very staunchly defended by its Confederate garrison. Above right: Fort Fisher after its capture by Federal forces.

THE CIVIL WAR: 1864

Above: artist's impression of a submarine attack on USS *Minnesota*. Blockaded by a superior fleet, the Confederates sought to redress the balance with a flotilla of submarines. A number of two- or four-man semi-submersible boats were built. These were known as "Davids" because of their intended role sinking Northern Goliaths. They were especially active in Charleston harbor, and on October 5, 1863, the U.S. ironclad *New Ironsides* was damaged, but not sunk. In the above picture the submarine is actually unarmed, since the artist has omitted to show the spar with its torpedo, which should be projecting from the bows. Left: photograph of a surviving "David," meant to be fully submerged.

Above: photograph of a semi-submersible "David," including the torpedo spar. Right: artist's impression of a crew at work inside a "David." The most spectacular submarine attack came on February 17, 1864, when the Confederate submarine *Hunley*, with a crew of eight, sank USS *Housatonic* in Charleston harbor (below right), making its attack on the surface and at night. It was a suicide attack, since the crew knew they were going to certain death. Five other crews had already drowned while preparing the boat and in training.

THE CIVIL WAR: 1864

The Confederate counter-blockade, mounted by commerce raiders attacking Union shipping, also suffered setbacks in 1864. The most successful commerce raider was CSS *Alabama,* whose two-year cruise cost the Union sixty-two ships. She was eventually sunk (left) when she attacked the heavier and better armed USS *Kearsarge* off the French coast on June 19. Below right: the officers of the *Kearsarge* on their ship soon after the battle. Captain John A. Winslow is third from the left.

Right: a typical Dahlgren naval gun, aboard the U.S. gunboat *Mendota.*

THE CIVIL WAR: 1864

Admiral David G. Farragut (left), the Civil War's finest exponent of naval warfare, was born in 1801 and was already serving at sea in the War of 1812, at the age of only only eleven years. In April 1862, he had run past the Mississippi batteries to capture New Orleans, later assisting the up-river campaigns against Port Hudson and Vicksburg. Then on August 5, 1864, he mounted a characteristically daring attack on the defences of Mobile Bay. When one of his monitors was sunk by a mine, he urged on the others with the immortal words "Damn the torpedoes. Go ahead." They did, and were rewarded with a completely successful operation.

Right: a map of the Gulf of Mexico and the Mississippi River, showing the theater of operations in the southwest.

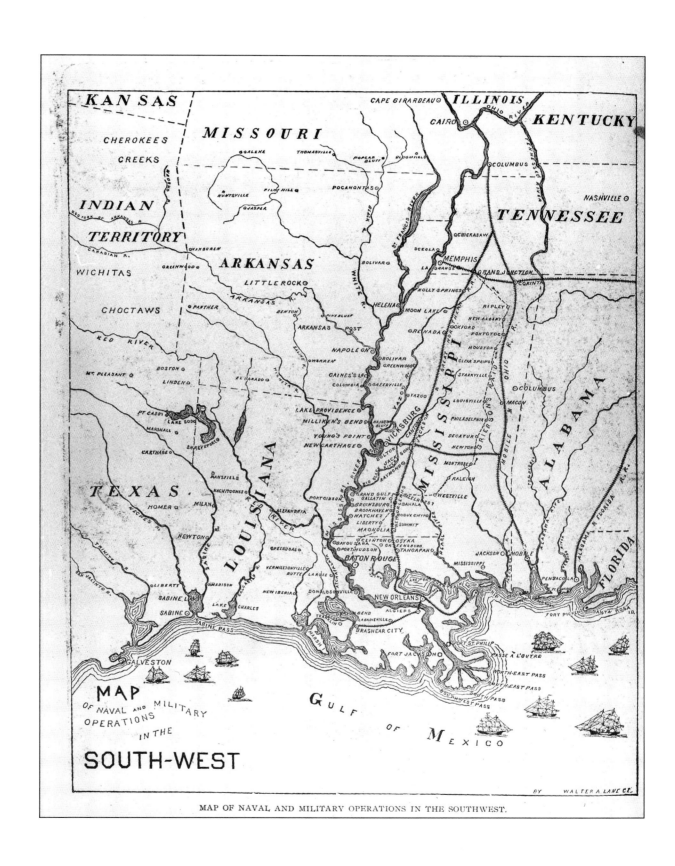

MAP OF NAVAL AND MILITARY OPERATIONS IN THE SOUTHWEST.

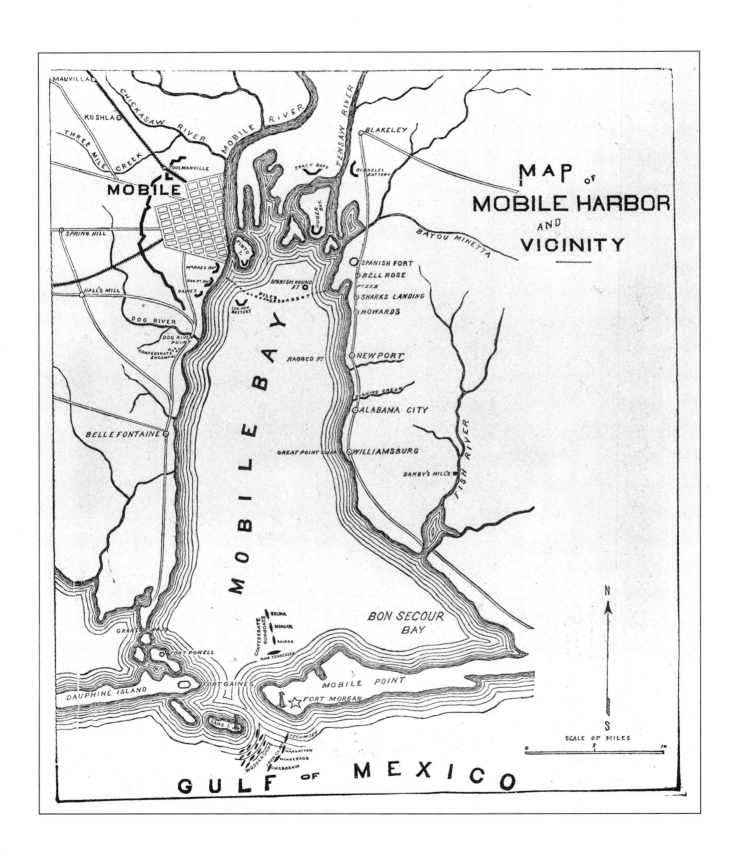

Left: a map of Mobile Harbor and its defenses, showing the dispositions of the two fleets on August 5, 1864. Right: the critical moment as Farragut's fleet enters Mobile Bay, running the gauntlet between Fort Morgan on the left and Fort Gaines on the right. The leading Union monitor *Tecumseh* has hit a mine and is sinking, while the Confederate ironclad *Tennessee* is entering the fray from the bottom left. It was in this desperate situation that Farragut's leadership saved the day. Below right: a painting by William A. Overend shows Farragut in action at Mobile.

Confederate soldiers would often try to get coffee, newspapers and greenbacks by trading with the enemy, using tobacco in particular, which was frequently unobtainable in the North.

Dressed beef hanging in a regimental commissary tent.

THE CIVIL WAR: 1864

The most important feature of camp life to a soldier was, of course, his food. The staple was hard army crackers (above) eaten with bacon, salted pork or quiveringly overfresh beef – and then more crackers. On the march there was always great interest in how many chickens might be stolen from each farm along the way, and corn or other vegetables could also often be found. The Union army had plenty of coffee, but the Confederates often had to make do with sorghum syrup.

Less amusing to the modern eye is a cock fight (right), photographed at General Orlando B. Wilcox's headquarters before Petersburg in August 1864.

THE CIVIL WAR
1865

The maze of trenchwork outside Petersburg was meant to compartmentalize each small group of soldiers in order to limit damage from enfilading fire. However, it also presented a serious obstacle to movement. Barbed wire was not invented until 1874, although on some occasions plain telegraph wire was used in Civil War fortifications. More usually, defensive entanglements would be made of wooden crisscrosses of chevaux-de-frise, such as can be seen in the background.

A victim of trench warfare, with a section of
chevaux-de-frise in the foreground.

THE CIVIL WAR: 1865

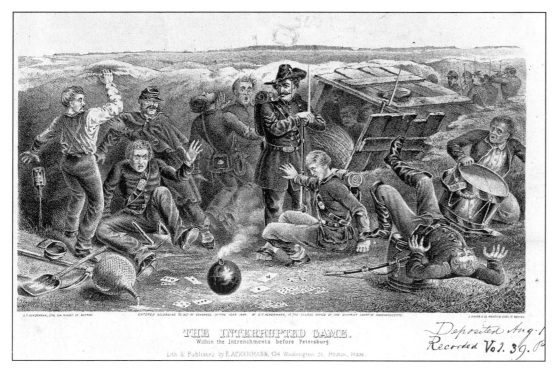

THE INTERRUPTED GAME.
Within the Intrenchments before Petersburg

Lith & Published by E. ACKERMANN, 134 Washington St. Boston, Mass.

Left: the effect of a mortar bomb on a card game in the Petersburg trenches. It was often noted in the Civil War that soldiers were addicted to cards, but would discard them before a big attack because of the moral stigma attached to them – no one wished to be killed while in possession of these instruments of the Devil. The threat of mortar bombs at Petersburg led to the building of bunkers (below left) with overhead cover. Right: Union infantry preparing to resume mobile operations before Petersburg. Lee hoped to make a breakout at Fort Stedman on March 25, 1865. Grant's spring offensive began six days later.

Left: the ruins of Richmond seen from across the James River.

Above: the first Union wagon train to enter Richmond at the beginning of April 1865.

THE CIVIL WAR: 1865

When Lee was finally outflanked and pushed back at Petersburg, he saw he must evacuate both the area and the capital. His army finally left Richmond on April 3 and the following morning the Mayor, Joseph C. Mayo, sent the following message to the Union forces outside the city: "The Army of the Confederate Government having abandoned the City of Richmond, I respectfully request that you will take possession of it with organized force, to preserve order and protect women and children and property." Unfortunately for law and order, the Union troops arrived too late to prevent widespread looting and destruction, which combined with planned official destruction of government property to create scenes of great carnage. Much of the city was destroyed by fire (right), leaving mournful ruins (remaining pictures) where so recently had stood the bustling capital of a proudly independent state.

THE CIVIL WAR: 1865

Federal soldiers pose on a locomotive (left) destroyed in Richmond, as big-game hunters might pose over their fallen prey. Below left: shot, shell and grape clusters in the ruins of the Tredegar iron works, Richmond. The works had been one of the foremost producers of munitions for the Confederate armies, and had worked wonders in almost meeting the heavy demand. Conversely, its destruction drove a major nail into the coffin of the Southern war effort. Right: cartoon mocking the continued defiance of Richmond ladies relying on U.S. rations amid the ruins of the city.

THE CIVIL WAR: 1865

After evacuating Richmond, Lee hoped to break out to the southwest, to join Johnston in North Carolina. Harried by Sheridan's cavalry and desperately short of supplies, however, he was headed off in a more westerly direction, and his already slender army withered away at an alarming rate. He hoped to feed it from four supply trains at Appomattox station, but when his vanguard arrived they found Sheridan's men already in possession, and the trains burned. Above: the remains of one of the trains.

Right: U.S. army officer of the Dragoons. In the Appomattox campaign, the Union cavalry came into its own as never before. It was used as a hard-hitting mobile spearhead to stake out claims for the infantry, rather than as the type of distant raiding force that had so often removed itself from the battlefield in the past.

With no way out of the trap, and his army reduced to just 13,000 men – less than the strength of an army corps – Lee was forced to make terms. In the parlor of the McClean home he sat down to talk (left and above) with Grant although, as he said, he "would rather die a thousand deaths." The terms they agreed provided for the soldiers of the Army of Northern Virginia to lay down their arms, pledge not to continue the fight, and disperse to their homes. Officers could keep their side arms, and men who owned horses could take them back to their farms.

We, the undersigned Prisoners of War, belonging to the Army of Northern Virginia, having been this day surrendered by General Robert E. Lee, C. S. A., Commanding said Army, to Lieut. Genl. U. S. Grant, Commanding Armies of United States, do hereby give our solemn parole of honor that we will not hereafter serve in the armies of the Confederate States, or in any military capacity whatever, against the United States of America, or render aid to the enemies of the latter, until properly exchanged, in such manner as shall be mutually approved by the respective authorities.

Done at Appomattox Court House, Va., this 9th day of April, 1865.

Right: Lee's signed parole. Below: sketch for a painting of the surrender of the Army of Northern Virginia to the Army of the Potomac.

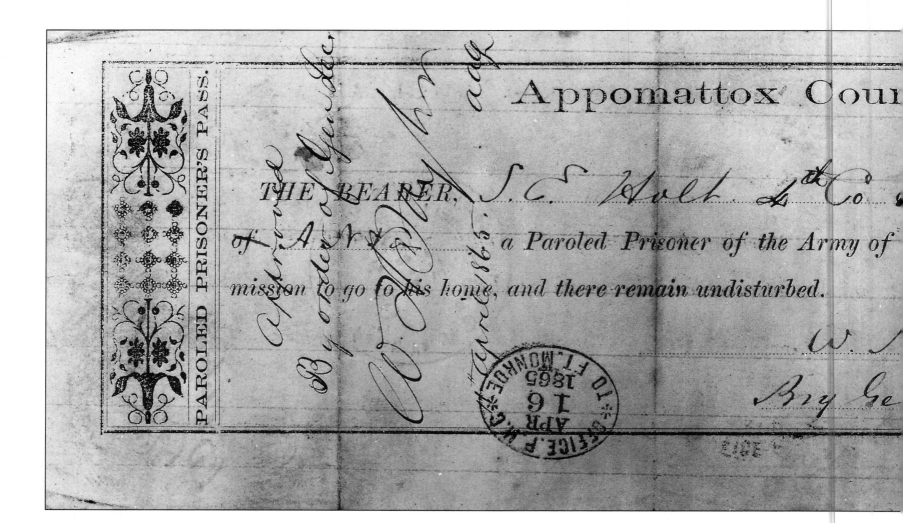

Above: passport for a paroled Confederate
prisoner of war, issued by the Union authorities
at Appomattaox.

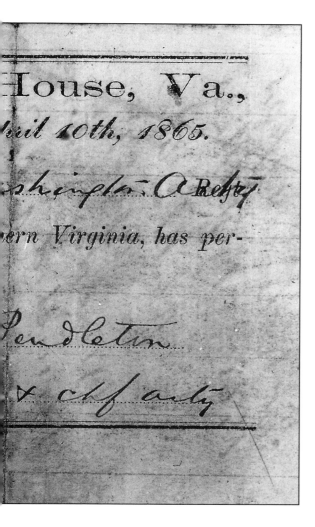

House, Va.,

il 10th, 1865.

shington Retfy

ern Virginia, has per-

Pendleton

& chf arly

While Sherman was marching through Georgia and the Carolinas, General James H. Wilson was preparing a massive all-cavalry raid through Alabama. Starting on March 22, 1865, this operation advanced deep into the state, defeating General Nathan B. Forrest at Selma. In order to make the raid possible, however, there had first been a major effort to collect horses from all possible sources. Right: a poster from Madison, Wisconsin, which reflects the shortage. Ironically it was only issued on the day that Wilson's campaign began.

2000 ARMY HORSES WANTED!

I want to purchase immediately at the Government Stables at this station,

TWO THOUSAND ARMY HORSES!

For which I will pay the prices named below, IN CASH. Horses must pass inspection under the following regulations, to wit :

FOR HORSES

Sound in all particulars, well broken, in full flesh and good condition, from fifteen (15) to sixteen (16) hands high, from five (5) to nine [9] years old, and well adapted in every way to Cavalry purposes—price

160 DOLLARS!

FOR HORSES

Of DARK Color, sound in all particulars, strong, quick and active, well broken, square trotters in harness, in good flesh and condition, from six [6] to ten [10] years old, not less than fifteen and one half [15 1-2] hands high, weighing not less than ten hundred and fifty [1050] pounds each, and adapted to Artillery service,

170 DOLLARS!

N. B. VAN SLYKE,

CAPT. & A. Q. M.

Assistant Quartermaster's Office, Madison, Wis., March 22, 1865.

THE CIVIL WAR: 1865

Sherman's march itself was unstoppable. On December 21, 1864, he entered Savannah, Georgia, but decided not to pursue the enemy army to Charleston, South Carolina. That city, the initial seat of the rebellion, had withstood repeated attacks from the coastal side, but in the process had been terribly battered (above) by artillery bombardments.

Instead of advancing along the coast, Sherman's spring campaign headed inland through Columbia and into North Carolina. Here he met General J. E. Johnston (left), who had been called out of retirement. He met and defeated him first in battle, at Bentonville on March 19, and then over the negotiating table, in the final surrender at Greensboro on April 26. Johnston greeted Sherman at Greensboro (below) as an old friend, using his familiar name "Cump" (for "Tecumseh"). Sherman for his part at first conceded far wider terms than anything the Washington government was prepared to tolerate – including allowing the troops to return, with their arms, to their own state capitals. Hasty disclaimers and denunciations were sent out by Edwin M. Stanton, who, following Lincoln's murder, had great authority in the government at that time. The final surrender terms were made very similar to those given to Lee in Virginia; but the bad blood between Sherman and Stanton was never forgotten.

Left: the arrest of Jefferson Davis, disguised as a woman, at Irwinville, Georgia, on May 10, 1865. He was imprisoned for two years, and a number of other senior Confederates were also jailed for varying spells, but the surrender terms at Appomattox and Greensboro ensured that there would be no widespread witch hunts.

The reality of camp life was rather more mundane than its lithographed image. A soldier of the 31st Pennsylvania Infantry (right) indicates by his saw that it involves plenty of forestry and excavation – but at least he is lucky enough to have both a tent, and his family in attendance! During most of the war, especially during mobile operations, such extravagances were almost unknown. The question was more one of whether an entire regiment could carry its baggage in one wagon or two.

Above and above right: Dr Bunnell's field embalming establishment at Fredericksburg, just after the battle. Many wealthy families – especially officers' families – would commission battlefield embalming and transportation of the deceased to his home town for burial in familiar surroundings.

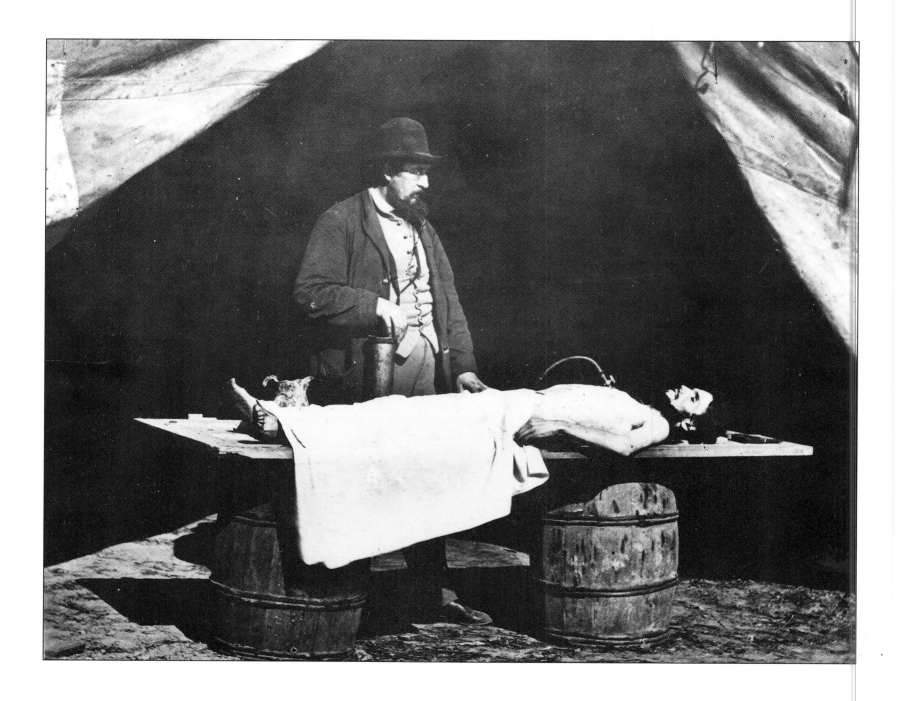

THE CIVIL WAR: 1865

The dead and nearly dead on the Civil War battlefields would be systematically "peeled," i.e. stripped (above), of all valuables, including clothes and especially boots. There are very few photographs of Civil War battle dead still wearing their boots.

A few days after a battle, most of the dead would be located, brought to central collecting points, then buried as quickly as possible. Normally this would be in unmarked graves, scattered almost randomly around the battlefield. In exceptional circumstances, as in Alexandria, Virginia (right), a formal soldiers' cemetery might be established, with consecrated ground and permanent headstones.

THE CIVIL WAR POSTWAR

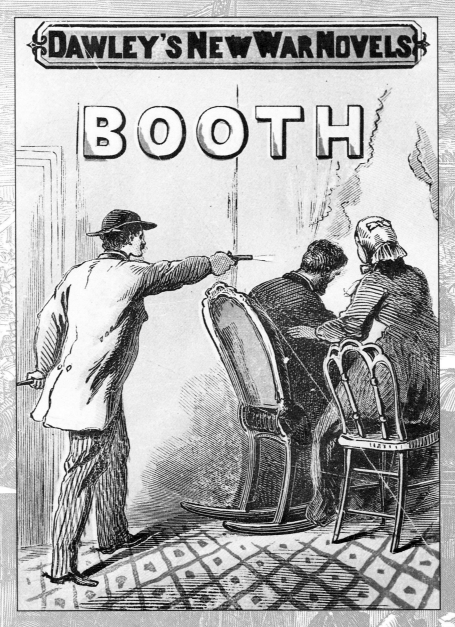

On April 14, 1865, less than a week after Lee had surrendered, but nearly two weeks before Johnston had done so, President Lincoln was shot in the back by John Wilkes Booth.

The Ford Theater in Washington, D.C., where Lincoln was watching the English comedy *Our American Cousin* when he was murdered shortly after ten in the evening, during the third act. Right: John Wilkes Booth, photographed before his crime. The son of a successful family of actors, he was actually an unsuccessful secessionist actor, who had hatched a plot with friends to assassinate several leading government figures. His most notorious performance had been suggested to him by his familiarity with the theater and its staff, and he added a few dramatic flourishes for effect. The assassin crept into the presidential box, fired his derringer, then jumped onto the stage and escaped, shouting the Virginia state motto *Sic Semper Tyrannis*. He was killed two weeks later while resisting arrest.

In the wake of Lincoln's assassination, Samuel Arnold (far left) and Edward Spangler (below far left) were jailed, and David E. Harold (left) and George Atzerodt (below center) were executed. Hartmann Richter (below), a cousin of George Atzerodt, was arrested on suspicion, but was not convicted.

Mary Surratt, George Atzerodt, Lewis Paine and David Harold were executed (above) on July 7, 1865. The fear of a widespread conspiracy tempted the authorities to take further far-reaching, strong measures, so it was perhaps fortunate that the relief of the newly won victory created a powerful pressure that quickly worked against more vindictive action or witch hunts. Nevertheless, books and articles alleging all manner of bizarre conspiracies continued to appear for several decades, accusing figures as diverse as Jefferson Davis and Vice President Andrew Johnson.

THE CIVIL WAR: 1865

Above: *The Soldier's Return*, a painting by A. D. O. Braviere that sums up the intense relief that swept both North and South when the killing stopped. Americans have never experienced a war that was so dangerous to its participants, either before or since.

Right: the return of the 69th New York Regiment to its home city, after a painting by Louis Lang. Consisting almost entirely of Irish soldiers, this outfit was perhaps welcomed home more warmly than most, because of these strong ethnic connections.

The Federal military occupation of the South was resented as a continuing alien presence in itself, but perhaps still more for the memory of Sherman's devastations. In one 1876 picture government troops (left) are still encamped in the South Carolina state capitol in Columbia, a town that had been almost totally destroyed during Sherman's passage. This is a propaganda picture, however. In reality, Federal troops in the South had been cut to barely 5,000 by this time.

As soon as the war was over, the South experienced an inrush of "carpetbaggers" (above) from all walks of life, looking for new political, economic or spiritual opportunities. Some were simply exploitative, others were genuinely anxious either to help, or to reform, or to guide. All of them, however, wanted to change things, and that was what the Southerners could not forgive.

Andrew Johnson (right) became the seventeenth U.S. President solely because he happened to be Vice President when Lincoln was murdered. He had little sympathy for the Republican mainstream, nor it for him. As a Southerner, he failed to send resolute signals to the former Confederacy, thereby helping reassure it that it did not need any radical modernization of outlook, when in reality it definitely did. Left: a cartoon, published in 1866, condemns his authoritarianism and his refusal to debate questions of importance with people of importance – a trait that was to lead to his impeachment in 1868. Above: another cartoon, published in the aftermath of the 1868 election campaign, gleefully prophesies that Johnson will soon be returning to the clothing trade from which he came.

RE-CONSTRUCTION,
OR "A WHITE MAN'S GOVERNMENT".

Johnson's early appeasement of the South had provoked Congress into a strong wave of civil rights measures in its revolt against him. This in turn had led to a white Southern backlash by the time General Grant took office as president in 1869. Few members of the Old South "establishment" could accept the degree or rapidity with which power within the local community was being transferred to carpetbaggers, "scalawags" and, especially, blacks (above).

Right: Northern cartoon for the 1868 presidential election, pointing out how little the political agenda of the South had been changed by the cessation of hostilities.

1864.   1868.
'TIS BUT A CHANGE OF BANNERS.

Above: two attorneys are "lacerated, boycotted and warned away" by the Ku Klux Klan. The Klan was conceived in Pulaski, Tennessee, on Christmas Eve 1865. It was at first intended as a type of social club for Confederate veterans, but the discovery that its masks and flowing robes could terrorize superstitious freed slaves soon brought it a far wider purpose. In 1867 in Nashville, it was more formally constituted as the "Invisible Empire of the South," whose aims embraced the clandestine social control of any elements found to be swimming against the tide of white Southern culture.

Right: Mississippi Klan "Warning" of 1871. The Klan quickly invented its own mumbo jumbo consistent with its ghostly image, and created a hierarchy of ranks with hydras, goblins, nighthawks, furies, and so on all the way up to a grand wizard, the first of whom was General Nathan B. Forrest, the brilliant cavalry raider of the Western theater. To his credit, Forrest tried to disband the Klan in 1869 because of its murders, kidnappings and lack of centralized discipline.

"Dam Your Soul. The Horrible *Sepulchre* and Bloody Moon has at last arrived. Some live to-day to-morrow "*Die.*" We the undersigned understand through our Grand "*Cyclops*" that you have recommended a big Black Nigger for Male agent on our nu rode; wel, sir, Jest you understand in time if he gets on the rode you can make up your mind to pull roape. If you have any thing to say in regard to the Matter, meet the Grand Cyclops and Conclave at Den No. 4 at 12 o'clock midnight, Oct. 1st, 1871.

"When you are in Calera we warn you to hold your tounge and not speak so much with your mouth or otherwise you will be taken on supprise and led out by the Klan and learnt to stretch hemp. Beware. Beware. Beware. Beware.

    (Signed)

                                                    "PHILLIP ISENBAUM,
                                                       "*Grand Cyclops*:
                                           "JOHN BANKSTOWN.
                                           "ESAU DAVES.
                                           "MARCUS THOMAS.
                                           "BLOODY BONES.

    "You know who. And all others of the Klan."

Facsimile of a Ku-Klux "Warning" in Mississippi—put in evidence before the Congressional Committee

These pages: press images of Ku Klux Klan killings between 1868 and 1871. In the North they created outrage, but in the South the murders often had precisely the effect their perpetrators had aimed for. Indeed, the civic and political powers that blacks had won in the late 1860s had been almost entirely negated by the late 1870s.

Plan of the Contemplated Murder of John Campbell.

Above: a press image of a planned Ku Klux Klan murder.

Right: an 1879 photograph showing black workers outside a barn used for cotton ginning. They were no longer slaves, but in many other respects the rights they had won in the 1860s had been almost totally whittled away.

THE CIVIL WAR: POSTWAR

The Civil War saw a great expansion of American industry, especially in modern production-line techniques, using interchangeable parts. The Colt gun factory (above) at Hartford, Connecticut, had led the way in this, but it also applied to many other high-technology items such as the clocks made at the Ingram works (above right) in Bristol, Connecticut. The problem for the South was that these new industries were already well established in the North, while whatever Southern factories had existed in 1861 had been systematically burnt down during the War.

Northern heavy industry was also booming, thanks to the railroad system (left) and its westward expansion. The postwar reconstruction of Southern railroads was certainly a great opportunity for the steel companies, but the unlimited prairies stretching to the Pacific Ocean represented a still greater one. Many skills and dollars that the South might otherwise have hoped to attract were thus diverted away to the West. The first transcontinental line was completed in 1869. One problem encountered by the railroads in the early years of reconstruction was the danger of armed robberies. Demobilized soldiers, especially those who had been Confederate raiders in the West, took to frontier lawlessness as a way of life. Particularly notorious was Jesse James, formerly a member of Quantrill's Kansas murder gang. He is pictured (right) with his brother Frank (seated) and a Confederate comrade on the left.

Left: portrait of Jesse James showing some of his extensive arsenal, his intense eyes and his haughty, high-boned face.

Whether "Wild" or otherwise, the West exerted a powerful magnetism on the many uprooted people that the war had created. The reconstruction period was a time of great change, and many families now decided to risk crossing the plains (right) to find new horizons nearer to the setting sun.

THE CIVIL WAR: POSTWAR

Ulysses S. Grant was commander of the Federal army during the later years of the Civil War and accepted the surrender of Robert E. Lee on April 9, 1865, at Appomattox Court House. He was elected as the eighteenth President of the United States in 1869 and he remained in the White House until 1877.